Dubai
Gateway to the Gulf

Edited by Ian Fairservice

MOTIVATE
PUBLISHING

Published by Motivate Publishing

Dubai: PO Box 2331, Dubai, UAE
Tel: (+971 4) 282 4060; fax: (+971 4) 282 0428
e-mail: books@motivate.ae www.booksarabia.com

Office 508, Building No 8, Dubai Media City, Dubai, UAE
Tel: (+971 4) 390 3550; fax: (+971 4) 390 4845

Abu Dhabi: PO Box 43072, Abu Dhabi, UAE
Tel: (+971 2) 677 2005; fax: (+971 2) 677 0124

London: Acre House, 11/15 William Road, London NW1 3ER
e-mail: motivateuk@motivate.ae

Directors: Obaid Humaid Al Tayer
                      Ian Fairservice

Consultant Editor: David Steele
Editor: Albert Harvey Pincis
Deputy Editor: Moushumi Nandy
Assistant Editor: Zelda Pinto
Senior Art Director: Fredrick Dittlau
Senior Designer: Cithadel Francisco
Designer: Charlie Banalo

General Manager Books: Jonathan Griffiths

Originally published 1986 as *The Commercial Book of Dubai*. Second edition 1987 as *Dubai –
Gateway to the Gulf*. Revised 1988 and 1990. Third edition 1991. Revised 1992, 1993 and
1994. Fourth edition 1997. Revised 1998 and 1999. Reprinted 1999. Fifth edition 2000 as
Dubai – Gateway 2000. Sixth edition 2001 as *Dubai – Gateway to the Gulf*. Seventh edition
2002. Reprinted 2003, 2004, 2005, 2006. Eighth edition 2007. Reprinted 2008

© Motivate Publishing 1986, 1991, 1997, 2000, 2001, 2002 and 2007

ISBN: 978 1 86063 224 2

British Library Cataloguing-in-Publication Data. A catalogue record for this book is available
from the British Library.

Printed by Rashid Printers & Stationers LLC, Ajman, UAE.

Photographic credits:

DP World: 22, 24, 25, 53
Dubai Autodrome: 73
Dubai Civil Aviation: 58
Dubai Duty Free: 77, 91
Dubai International Financial
   Centre: 31
Dubai Shopping Festival: 28, 90
Dubai World Central: 59
Emirates: 52, 60
Gallo Images/Getty Images: 70

Gulf Images: 32, 84
Jumeirah: 1, 72, 75T, 78B, Back cover
Motivate Publishing: 51
   Duncan Chard: 4, 37
   Fadi Gwanny: 34
   Karel Kita: 29, 33, 35
   Greg Newington: 6/7, 57, 63, 75B
   Sheldon Pereira: 97, 98
   Farooq Salik: 69, 96
   Adiseshan Shanker: 76R

Callaghan Walsh: 71, 76L
Nakheel: 42
Space Imaging Middle East: 40
David Steele: 8, 9, 10, 11, 13, 14, 15,
   16, 17, 18, 19, 20, 21, 26, 38, 39,
   41, 43, 45, 47, 48T&B, 49, 50, 55,
   56, 61, 64, 65, 66, 67, 68, 78T,
   81T&B, 83, 86, 87, 89T&B, 95, 101
Andrea Willmore: 85, 92

His Highness Sheikh Mohammed bin Rashid Al Maktoum, Vice-President
and Prime Minister of the UAE and Ruler of Dubai.

Introduction

by His Highness Sheikh Hasher Al Maktoum
Director General, Department of Information
Government of Dubai

Dubai has established itself as the first port of call in the Gulf for businessmen and tourists, a vital trading link between East and West. For centuries dhows have plied the waters of the Gulf and reached distant shores in Asia and Africa. Today, Dubai is still a major trading centre and the business life of our city is as diverse as it is prosperous.

Under the guidance of His Highness Sheikh Rashid bin Saeed Al Maktoum, who ruled Dubai from 1958–1990, Dubai entered the modern era, developing a world-class infrastructure financed through oil revenues. It also earned itself an enviable trading position, becoming the leading re-export centre of the region. These achievements were built on by Sheikh Rashid's sons and successors, the late Sheikh Maktoum bin Rashid Al Maktoum and by the current Vice-President and Prime Minister of the United Arab Emirates and Ruler of Dubai, Sheikh Mohammed bin Rashid Al Maktoum.

Dubai has harnessed the latest developments in technology. Our communications and transport systems now complete an enviable infrastructure. Since October 1985 Dubai has been the home of Emirates airline, offering further evidence of Dubai's vital role in linking the Gulf with the rest of the world. Industrial development has continued to increase, major contributors being the port of Jebel Ali and the Jebel Ali Free Trade Zone (JAFZA).

However, one of the most important sectors of our economy today is tourism. In addition to its excellent hotels which offer first-class leisure facilities, Dubai hosts a range of sporting events that appeal to visitors throughout the year. The annual Dubai Desert Classic attracts world-class golfers and golfing enthusiasts, while the Dubai Tennis Championships bring in international tennis players and draw large crowds. Dubai is also the home of the world's richest horse race, the Dubai World Cup. Other major sporting events include powerboat racing, motor rallying and rugby.

The Dubai Shopping Festival, inaugurated in 1996, encapsulates the entrepreneurial spirit of Dubai and occupies a whole month in the emirate's busy calendar of events. In addition to the special retail promotions, it provides entertainment ranging from street parades to firework displays. A similar annual festival, Dubai Summer Surprises, attracts throngs of visitors in summer.

This book gives an excellent account of the commercial, industrial and financial life of our city and also documents its many cultural, sporting and tourist attractions. Through this publication you will also learn something of the history of our land, its heritage and its people.

Despite its modernity, Dubai holds fast to time-honoured principles and traditions, including that of hospitality for which the Arab World is renowned. I am delighted to welcome you to Dubai and invite you to experience first hand the many and varied aspects of our beautiful emirate.

Front Cover: Traditional trading dhows moored alongside Dubai Creek, with the Dubai Chamber of Commerce & Industries and the National Bank of Dubai buildings in the background.

Back cover: A Bedouin with his camels at Bab Al Shams Desert Resort and Spa.

Left: Emirates Towers have been a Dubai landmark since the beginning of the new millennium.

Following spread: Many attractive wilderness areas are within a couple of hours drive from the centre of Dubai.

Contents

Chapter One
The United Arab Emirates

Abu Dhabi is the capital city of the UAE and is situated on an island.

For 5,000 years, the inhabitants of the lower Gulf survived on fishing, hunting, harvesting dates and herding sheep and goats, with luxuries provided by trading commodities such as pearls and copper.

Then, in the space of one lifetime, this harsh and difficult existence was transformed beyond all recognition, as the sagacious investment of oil wealth resulted in a life of luxury within garden cities that boast the very best of man's ingenuity. Though oil was discovered in 1958 off the coast of Abu Dhabi, it was not until the 1960s that it began to be exported from what is now the United Arab Emirates (UAE), with Dubai also exporting oil by the end of the decade.

At that time, the region was still essentially a tribal society of seven independent sheikhdoms, collectively known as the Trucial States because of their maritime agreements with Britain. This status dated back to the early part of the 19th century when Britain enforced a maritime peace treaty to ensure the safe passage of its ships to and from India.

In 1968, Britain announced it was withdrawing from the region. At that time, the seven sheikhdoms had a total population of 180,000 people scattered across 90,600 square kilometres of desert and mountain. Today, the population of the UAE exceeds four-million people with some 80 per cent of Dubai's population of more than 1.2 million being made up of expatriates, predominantly from the Indian subcontinent, but also including other Asians, Arabs and Westerners.

What made this desert region suddenly so attractive, and how did this astonishing transformation come about?

The two leading sheikhdoms, Abu Dhabi and Dubai, realized that by combining the individual sheikhdoms, they could create a strong federation. In 1971, led by Sheikh Zayed bin Sultan Al Nahyan, then Ruler of Abu Dhabi, and Sheikh Rashid bin Saeed Al Maktoum, then Ruler of Dubai, and joined by Ajman, Fujairah, Sharjah and Umm al-Qaiwain, the United Arab Emirates was formed. Ra's al-Khaimah joined the following year. Foreign affairs, defence and social services became

Trading dhows moored in Dubai Creek – the main artery of a dynamic city.

Sharjah, the cultural capital of the UAE, is also a city that plays a leading role in the economic development of the region.

federal concerns, while each emirate retained autonomy over its internal affairs.

Following this union, the UAE built on its strengths. Oil revenues were employed to fund an impressive infrastructure that today includes superbly equipped modern hospitals, well-maintained multi-lane carriageways, highly efficient international seaports, busy international airports, top-class hotels and beach resorts, and superb air-conditioned shopping malls, among other numerous one-of-a-kind developments. The quality of infrastructure in turn facilitated further trade, building on the expertise of the local population.

The UAE now has one of the highest per-capita incomes in the world, which is reflected by economic successes and a quality of life envied by many.

Abu Dhabi and Al Ain

In 1761, according to legend, hunters of the Bani Yas tribe from the Liwa oases followed a gazelle across a shallow channel to a coastal island where they discovered a freshwater spring. The island was named Abu Dhabi (Father of the Gazelle) and the tribe later established a fishing village on the coast, the precursor to the modern city of Abu Dhabi, capital of the emirate and also of the federation. In fact, man had settled near the site far earlier, as the 4,000-year-old archaeological remains found on the nearby island of Umm al-Nar and elsewhere testify.

Some of today's inhabitants can recall when this glistening metropolis was no more than a white fort on the edge of a cluster of barasti (palm-frond) huts. Much of Abu Dhabi's history is linked to the sea and this link is still celebrated on national and religious holidays with picturesque sailing dhow and rowing-boat races off the capital's Corniche.

Inland, some 160 kilometres east of Abu Dhabi, is the oasis city of Al Ain, where the stark Hajar Mountains meet the desert plains, and water springs forth to feed beautiful oases. Here, in Hili Archaeological Gardens, a magnificent carved tomb some 5,000 years old demonstrates that, even inland, this corner of Arabia was inhabited in prehistoric times.

While the tomb has been restored and other Bronze Age archaeological remains have been made accessible, Al Ain is probably better known today for its numerous forts, oases and parks, as well as its zoo, university, museum and fun fair. It is also the hometown of the UAE's late President, Sheikh Zayed, who was previously a revered governor of the region; it was under his guidance that the city developed so rapidly.

Another inland area of Abu Dhabi is the Liwa, the ancestral home of the ruling Al Nahyan family for at least two centuries. The Liwa is formed by a crescent of scattered mini-oases, each settlement originally comprising just a few mud houses and a scattering of date palms. Now even this remote corner, once seen only by the Bedouin and a handful of explorers, has been touched by development, with tarred highways and weekend trippers exploring the magnificent dunes of the adjacent Rub al-Khali (The Empty Quarter).

The Northern Emirates

North of Dubai are the five remaining emirates. The nearest, just 13 kilometres along the coast, is Sharjah, which has an area of some 2,600 square kilometres. For the past 300 years, it has been ruled by the Al Qasimi family, once considered the greatest Arab maritime power in the Gulf.

At one time, Sharjah was the main town in what is now the UAE, site of a fort-cum-airport for passengers stopping over en route to India. It is also the site of the country's first school. Sharjah's importance declined when its creek silted up and larger vessels stopped at Dubai instead but, with a population exceeding 750,000 it's once again a significant part of the country.

Oil was discovered in Sharjah in 1974 and gas in 1980, facilitating an economic revival, and the emirate has successfully pursued a combined course of encouraging light industry and beautification projects ever since. Among the many examples of distinctive architecture are the emirate's evocative souks and modern buildings incorporating Islamic influences. New souks along traditional lines have been built in the city of Sharjah, and also in Dhaid, Khor Fakkan and Dibba. These last two sites are enclaves of Sharjah on the East Coast of the UAE, popular with tourists and weekend trippers seeking a more leisurely pace of life.

Alternating with sections of Sharjah territory on the East Coast is the Emirate

One of the seven emirates that make up the UAE, Fujairah boasts some of the best scenery in the country as well as several magnificent forts.

of Fujairah, which covers an area totalling some 1,300 square kilometres, made up of mountain and coastal plain. Effectively cut off from the rest of the country until a decade ago, when a tarred road from Masafi was constructed, Fujairah has a quiet charm of its own with traditional mud forts, fishing villages and date plantations fed by *aflaj* (irrigation channels).

Today, Fujairah also has a trade centre, a thriving port and an international airport, part of a strategy to increase its revenues from tourism. The town is dominated by a magnificent old fort that, until recently, bore the scars of a British naval bombardment in 1920.

Back on the Gulf coast are the emirates of Ajman and Umm al-Qaiwain, both developed from fishing villages, an inheritance demonstrated today by Umm al-Qaiwain being the site of a fishing research centre, and Ajman having the largest dhow-building yard in the country. Each emirate also has its own historic forts.

Ra's al-Khaimah, which borders Oman's Musandam Peninsula, has a rich history, and it too once had a period of pre-eminence. It's the site of the lost city of Julfar, which flourished until the 18th-century AD when it was abandoned and forgotten. The town's historical fort is now one of the best museums in the country.

Ra's al-Khaimah's 1,700 square kilometres are mostly mountainous, and the emirate enjoys relatively good water supplies from the Hajar Mountains, permitting a well-developed agricultural sector that even produces strawberries for export to Europe. Its industries include quarrying and pharmaceuticals; there's also a port, and limited hydrocarbon reserves are now being exploited.

Apart from being the most rugged of the emirates, Ra's al-Khaimah also offers attractions such as hot springs, hidden date plantations and abandoned villages. Yet its main town features many modern amenities, including quality hotels and an international airport. The coastline is rich in marine life and is especially popular with divers.

Achievements of the UAE

Since Federation, the United Arab Emirates has achieved a high standard of living, with its residents enjoying one of the world's highest per-capita income levels, steadily remaining above US$21,000 in recent years.

In addition to its citizens' physical well-being, their spiritual needs are also being met with a massive mosque-building programme reaching virtually every residential and business district, as well as schemes to promote an understanding of Islam and the Holy Qur'an.

The older generation has adjusted remarkably well to the changes all around – more than 100,000 have benefited from literacy schemes established for those that did not have the opportunity to go to school. The new generation has no such worries. Although the Emirates' first school opened in Sharjah in 1953, the country now has a highly developed educational system. UAE nationals are now able to acquire the skills and education to be able to fully play their parts as productive members of a dynamic and forward-thinking society.

The UAE also has an impressive number of universities, offering a wide range of degree courses, located in Abu Dhabi, Ajman, Al Ain, Dubai and Sharjah. In addition, there are 12 campuses of the Higher Colleges of Technology, providing professional training for young nationals preparing to enter the workforce, as well as other specialized training establishments such as Dubai Aviation College. With the development of Dubai Knowledge Village (DKV), Dubai has established itself as a centre for higher learning and innovation, offering fully accredited degree programmes and research and development centres. DKV is set to expand to include a mega-campus called Dubai Knowledge Universities, which has already attracted top universities to set up campuses.

Built at the turn of the new millennium, the imposing Sheikh Zayed Mosque overlooks the attractive *khor*, or creek, of Ra's al-Khaimah.

Chapter Two
The Land, its Heritage and People

The UAE can be divided into three main natural areas: the coastal plains, the desert interior (dunes and gravel plains) and the mountains.

A patchwork of independent sheikhdoms joined together in December 1971 to forge a sovereign state in a desert and mountain peninsula, becoming the United Arab Emirates.

Formerly part of the Trucial States, the country now consists of seven independent emirates: Abu Dhabi, Dubai, Sharjah, Ajman, Umm al-Qaiwain, Ra's al-Khaimah and Fujairah. The name Trucial States refers to the maritime truces established between the emirates and the British during the 19th century. The ending of treaty agreements with the British in 1971 coincided with the boost in world oil prices. Consequently, the oil-rich emirates were able to flourish and prosper under the leadership of a number of strong-willed men, most noticeably Sheikh Zayed, Sheikh Rashid and the rulers of the other emirates.

Sheikh Rashid is acknowledged as the 'Father of Modern Dubai' and his visionary work was continued by Sheikh Maktoum bin Rashid Al Maktoum until his untimely death early in 2006. Sheikh Maktoum was succeeded by his brother, HH Sheikh Mohammed bin Rashid Al Maktoum, who took up the posts of UAE Vice-President and Prime Minister, and Ruler of Dubai, while retaining his portfolio of UAE Minister of Defence.

Since 1971 the country has seen a pace of progress unequalled almost anywhere in the world. Seemingly overnight highways and health facilities, schools and universities, electricity and water plants, housing and hotels, sports facilities of every kind, satellite stations and cement factories, airports and office complexes, shopping malls and exhibition centres, beach complexes and grassed golf courses, publishing houses and television studios, have sprung up.

All these ventures were undertaken at the same time as the diplomatic feat of knitting together, into a federal whole, seven fiercely independent emirates – an amazing triumph by any standard.

The years since federation are but the blink of an eye compared with the earlier history of what was to become the UAE. Before the arrival of modern communications the area was isolated: to the south lay the forbidding wastes of the Rub al-Khali, The Empty Quarter; to the east rose the Hajar Mountains, a jagged spine of sun-baked rocks; and to the north and west the Arabian Gulf. Yet despite this apparent disadvantage, those early inhabitants developed a complex and, for the time, sophisticated society of settled communities.

Archaeologists tell us that around 5,000 years ago the local inhabitants possessed both the time and wealth to acquire personal items far beyond those of a subsistence economy. 'How did those ancient desert dwellers achieve this?' asks the visitor, who at first glance sees only a harsh, inhospitable landscape beyond the modern cities.

Dubai's old merchant quarter of Bastikiya has been carefully renovated and is especially note-worthy for its splendid examples of wind-towers.

Arab women wearing traditional dress enjoy a summer stroll among flame trees in Dubai's popular Safa Park.

Admittedly, it's believed that the climate was kinder then, permitting the development of agriculture and animal husbandry. Even more important was the UAE's position on the trade routes between Oman and Yemen in the far south and the flourishing Sumerian civilization of the fertile crescent of the Euphrates and Tigris valleys in the north-west. Even the imposing barrier of the Hajar Mountains harboured minerals such as copper, needed by the Sumerian cities.

In more recent times it's still been trade that's featured prominently in the economy of the UAE in general and Dubai in particular. Dubai's Creek provided one of the few safe anchorages along the southern coast of the Gulf, a haven for the dhows that cleaved the blue waters of the Arabian Sea, returning from their voyages with holds full of cardamom, cinnamon, cloves, sandalwood and timber.

Nowadays the Creek also plays host to pleasure craft, and its banks are lined by the mirrored glass and concrete of more modern trading and financial establishments, whose communications are by satellite rather than sail. The same waters lap the 21st-century quayside and still splash the walls of the wind-towered houses of the merchants of a bygone era, providing a pleasing sense of continuity.

For the people of Dubai – residents, business travellers and tourists – the Creek holds a special attraction, similar to other historic waterways that are the pivotal landmark of great metropolises around the world.

Progress charting

It's perhaps these pervasive links with the past that gives Dubai its unique flavour.

In the development of any city – and particularly one that's also a port – it's important that nature be permitted a voice in the sessions of the planning committees, for it is only by allowing this that subsequent generations may chart the progress of their town and feel themselves to be a part of its growth, while still retaining the essential links with their heritage. Happily, the Creek is still at the heart of Dubai today.

The waterway has quietly flowed through much of Dubai's history. It was the starting and finishing point for pearling expeditions that, until the worldwide recession and the introduction of the cultured pearl in the 1930s, formed a vital part of the economy. Some 3,000 vessels were employed in the trade, leaving harbour in May and not returning until mid-September. Hardy men they were indeed. While their vessels were anchored off the great pearl bank in the relentless heat of summer, they lived on a frugal diet of dates, fish, rice and coffee, and made up to 50 dives a day.

Fishing too was, and still is, an important activity, with the warm and shallow waters of the Arabian Gulf supporting a wide diversity of marine life. And, continuing this seafaring history, even today dhows are built locally, using the materials and methods practised by generations of boat builders.

Trade is still Dubai's raison d'être. Oil revenues have financed the expansion of business, and local industries related to oil form a very important segment of the economy. But it's the buying and selling of goods, ports and airports, tourism, finance and the real-estate market that is the key to Dubai's present success and future prosperity.

The Heritage Village in Shindagha is the place to visit for an insight into the time-honoured lifestyles of the region.

17

Dance and music remain paramount in Dubai's culture. Here a group perform the *ayyala* – the stick dance which started as a response to danger.

Enduring traditions

Most UAE citizens still wear the traditional dress; for men the *dishdasha* (the long, flowing white robe) so practical for this climate; for women it's still customary to wear the black *abaya* that covers them from head to foot. Occasionally, especially among the older women, the *abaya* is accompanied by the *burqa*, a leather mask that covers the mouth and nose. Even so, the wearers of these centuries-old garments still shop in the most fashionable boutiques and drive the latest cars on a highway system that, once major road works and a new light railway system are completed, will be the envy of many a 'developed' country. All this may sound incongruous to visitors before they arrive but, in fact, the seamlessness of combining the old with the new is the memory that lingers.

Among traditional sports, camel racing, probably offering the ultimate in spectator participation, is something of a national passion. On formal racecourses in the cities, or on the more casual tracks in the country, races are followed with fervour. There's no betting, however, for the owners are gambling with something more precious than money; it's their pride of ownership that is at stake.

More than 30 camels race on courses of up to eight kilometres long. This in itself is exciting enough, but the owners and spectators join in too, following the progress of their favourite racing camel in 4x4 vehicles amid clouds of dust, a cacophony of horns and wild exhortations.

Falconry, too, is an ancient and noble sport still enjoyed in the UAE. Probably founded in the rolling steppes of central Asia, it grew in importance in Arabia following the Muslim conquests that brought the Arabs into contact with the Byzantine Empire.

What has not changed is the renowned Arab hospitality. The ancient custom of the desert, where every visitor or traveller is considered an honoured guest, is still every bit as true today, whether it be in a social or business environment.

The considerably more brusque Western approach may offer a marginal increase in efficiency, but the Arab method is far more gracious and probably produces, in the end, an infinitely more satisfactory exchange. Even if it doesn't, it can be a pleasant alternative to regular Western business practices.

Dining is another aspect of life that successfully combines East and West. The traditional whole lamb served on a bed of rice is still much in evidence both in hotels and private houses. So too is just about any other type of food, from Japanese and Chinese cuisines via French haute cuisine and Italian pasta to American fast food or Mexican tacos.

The first-time visitor arriving at one of the UAE's sophisticated international airports is quickly whisked along modern boulevards in the comfort of an air-conditioned taxi to a luxury hotel. He or she could be forgiven for thinking that Dubai was just another busy city, full of handsome architecture and leafy parks displaying all the comforts of contemporary life. Such a visitor would be partly right, but would also be missing an essential element.

For all its Western aspects, the UAE is still very much an Arab country. The mosques are undeniably beautiful, but they do not exist as mere decoration. They represent a real, fundamental religious code of such scope and detail that it en-compasses and provides guidance and comfort in every aspect of life. This is per-haps the key to the outstanding success of the UAE. From deep inner security springs the ability to welcome the stranger, no matter where he or she is from, and to deal with the challenges of change. *Ahlan wa sahlan*. Welcome from the heart.

Dubai owes much of its prosperity and character to the sea and the spirit of the Arab mariner lives on in the emirate's glorious racing dhows.

Chapter Three
Commerce

Trading dhows have moored in Dubai Creek for centuries, the only difference being that they are now powered by motors rather than sail.

Although Dubai has been at the centre of trading activities in the Gulf for centuries, it was less than 150 years ago that its position was recognized by the international community. In the late 1870s, Britain declared Dubai the principal port of the Trucial States and a centre for the import and export of goods by British merchants.

The Bombay and Persia Steam Navigation Company originally used the port of Sharjah as its base but, in 1890, was persuaded that Dubai had more to offer. The company transferred its operations to Dubai and initially used the port for mail delivery. By 1905, 34 steamers were calling regularly at Dubai, and the annual volume of cargo quickly rose to 70,000 tonnes.

It was not too long before the merchants and traders of India realized the potential that existed in Dubai. Cheap passenger fares on the regular steamer from Bombay to Dubai soon brought in more traders, and importers set up their stalls in the commercial areas of Dubai and across the Creek, in Deira.

The twin foundations

For decades, fortunes were made from trading pearls and gold. The pearling industry of Dubai was renowned around the world and, even today, Dubai pearls are treasured by royalty and have been nestled away in private collections in

European and Asian countries.

The trade in gold was also the basis of many fortunes in early Dubai, with much of the trade coming from the subcontinent. Indian gold prices were fixed at a higher rate than the free market and several of today's great merchant traders owe their success to astute gold trading in the early part of the century.

Today, the original gold souks of Deira can still be visited, although a newer gold souk now stands on a site overlooking the Creek and there's a new gold-and-diamond centre off Sheikh Zayed Road. Whether old or new, a thriving gold trade persists in Dubai, not least because of a continuing demand from India. This demand is so great that, until recently, London banks exported more gold to Dubai than almost anywhere else in the world, except Switzerland.

Sadly for many, the Western demand for pearls had decreased as the Great Depression of 1929–1934 dug in. Then, as if this blow was not already enough, the Japanese introduced the cheaper cultured pearl and, at the end of the 1930s, the world plunged into war. The pearling industry would never recover.

As is often the case in Dubai, the end of one era witnessed the start of another. During the 1930s oil, which had previously been discovered in Iran, Iraq and Bahrain, was discovered in Kuwait, Qatar and Saudi Arabia. It was discovered off Abu Dhabi in 1958 and smaller reserves were found in Dubai territory in 1966, in the Fateh offshore field, 90 kilometres west of the town.

Modern buildings, such as those of the National Bank of Dubai (left) and the Dubai Chamber of Commerce & Industry, overlook Dubai Creek.

Three years later, in 1969, oil exports began from Dubai when a tanker took delivery of 180,000 barrels of crude. Although significant, Dubai's oil reserves have always been a fraction of those of Abu Dhabi and today – perhaps to the surprise of many readers – account for less than eight per cent of the emirate's GDP.

Even though the discovery of oil brought about massive change, it would be a mistake to think that Dubai was an economic backwater before the first oil was exported. The past four decades have borne witness to amazing growth in commerce. Official figures illustrate the dramatic story. In 1958, imports to Dubai were valued at just US$5.7 million (Dhs 21 million). Millions soon become billions, as the discovery of oil and gas in the 1960s fuelled massive economic growth. By 1990, imports had risen to US$1.1 billion (Dhs 4 billion) a year and, by 2004, to nearly US$4 billion (Dhs 15 billion) with China, India, Japan, the United States, Germany, the United Kingdom, France, Switzerland, Italy and South Korea the top 10 on the list of supplier countries.

Much of the import bill goes to meet the needs not only of a fast-expanding economy, but also of an ever-increasing population. As the 'land of promise', Dubai continues to attract expatriate workers from all corners of the globe, with the result that the emirate's population has more than tripled in the past 20 years – from a total of 419,000 in 1985 to more than 1.2 million people according to an official census conducted late in 2005. Today, the total population of the UAE stands at more than four million people, an increase of 40 per cent in little more than 10 years.

Dubai currently re-exports goods to more than 120 countries and is a vital part of the trade community. India is currently the biggest market, followed by Iran, Iraq, Switzerland, Pakistan, Algeria, Belgium, Honk Kong, Libya, Saudi Arabia and the United States.

The re-export business benefits from the successful operation of Dubai's two main ports, Port Rashid and Jebel Ali. In 1991 these two ports were combined under one overall administrative body, the Dubai Ports Authority and, in 2001, merged with more authorities to form the Ports, Customs and Free Zone

Inaugurated in 1979, Jebel Ali Port, adjacent to Jebel Ali Free Zone, was voted the 'best seaport in the Middle East' for the 12th consecutive year in 2006.

Corporation. Since then steady growth has helped consolidate the corporation's position as the biggest container port in the Middle East and one of the largest in the world.

A steady expansion of facilities for handling non-container cargo, combined with a marketing drive in newly emerging economies around the world, continue to fuel growth in both cargo volumes and the number of shipping lines (currently totalling more than 125) using Port Rashid and Jebel Ali.

Dubai is also one of the world's leading air-cargo centres. The purpose-built Dubai Cargo Village, a US$75 million project when it opened at Dubai International Airport in 1991, was initially capable of handling 250,000 tonnes per year. That capacity was quickly overtaken, however, as cargo volumes grew apace: facilities have been under constant expansion ever since.

The Cargo Village has now outgrown its facilities and is undergoing a US$200 million expansion. Depending on growth and projections, the existing cargo terminal will be demolished and replaced by the final phase of the four-phase Mega-Terminal, capable of handling a capacity of 2.7 million tonnes per year and set for completion in 2018. In addition to all these developments, the new Dubai World Central International Airport near Jebel Ali will be able to handle an additional 12 million tonnes of cargo a year. (For more on Dubai's ports, Cargo Village and Dubai World Central International Airport, see next chapter.)

Although re-exports account for much of Dubai's outgoing trade, direct exports continue to grow with India and the United States the biggest buyers, mainly of base metals. Completing the top 10 major export markets are Iran, Taiwan, Iraq, Yemen, Japan, Pakistan, Saudi Arabia and Indonesia.

Free trade

The Government of Dubai is consistent in following a free-trade policy and import duties have remained at four per cent for many years.

Thanks to the foresight of Sheikh Rashid, the Jebel Ali Free Zone Authority

The discovery of oil in the Fateh offshore field brought about massive change but, today, oil accounts for only eight per cent of Dubai's GDP.

Jebel Ali Free Zone was built around the port of Jebel Ali. More than 100 shipping lines use Jebel Ali and Port Rashid.

(JAFZA) was established. He decreed that it remain duty free and that 100-per-cent foreign ownership of companies be allowed – a policy carried forward by his sons and successors, Sheikh Maktoum and Sheikh Mohammed (for more on JAFZA, see next chapter).

The development of JAFZA followed the decision by customs directors of the Arab Gulf Cooperation Council (AGCC) in 1985 to abolish double taxation of goods re-exported from a member country. For Dubai's merchant community, it opened up markets in Bahrain, Kuwait, Oman, Qatar and Saudi Arabia. Since the implementation of this in 1987, Dubai's re-export trade has strengthened and trans-shipment routes now extend throughout the Middle East and as far afield as Central Asia and South Africa.

Although Dubai has successfully developed its commerce to enjoy all the benefits of modern methods, as witnessed by the twin ports and a booming air-cargo facility, traditional trade by dhow continues unabated. Hundreds of these traditional wooden vessels still ply the ocean routes from their berths along Dubai Creek and at Al Hamriyah Port. Al Hamriyah was inaugurated in 1976 with docking facilities for dhows of all sizes. In the 1970s, dhow traffic was responsible for two-thirds of Dubai's imports for re-export. Although that percentage has undoubtedly declined, dhow traffic remains an important part of Dubai's

commerce and will continue to play a role for many years to come.

Dubai World Trade Centre

Established more than a quarter of a century ago in 1979, the Dubai World Trade Centre (DWTC) has become a focal point for business interests in the Middle East. The centre encompasses a broad range of facilities, all aimed at supporting Dubai's goal to become an international business hub and first-class international destination for the lucrative meetings, incentives, conventions and exhibitions (MICE) industry in the 21st century.

Located alongside Sheikh Zayed Road – Dubai's busiest highway and main artery to Abu Dhabi – the 39-storey Trade Centre Tower is a landmark in the region and in its early days was the tallest building in the Middle East. It's regarded as a monument to Sheikh Rashid, who had the vision to construct the tower.

To confirm its role as the leading exhibition and event venue in the Middle East, DWTC has undergone much expansion and has significantly extended its range of facilities, with the construction of the new Dubai International Convention Centre (DICC), completed in 2003, in time to host the 58th Board of Governors' Meetings of the International Monetary Fund and World Bank. The convention centre is large enough to accommodate events hosting up to 11,000

Port Rashid is situated adjacent to the mouth of Dubai Creek and caters for ships that are too large to enter the Creek.

delegates and the expansion programme included the construction of two hotels and a 13-storey office tower.

The DICC changed its name to the Dubai International Convention and Exhibition Centre (DICEC) when a 15,000-square-metre exhibition hall was added in 2005 to accommodate the phenomenal growth of the MICE industry.

As Dubai evolves, so too does DWTC. During the next few years, some components of the current DWTC complex adjacent to Sheikh Zayed Road will be demolished and a complex of 40 buildings extending from the DWTC Tower to Jumeirah Emirates Towers will replace it. The new DWTC complex will include a state-of-the-art convention centre, office and residential towers, hotels and hotel apartments, shopping facilities, and links to Dubai's metro system, which is scheduled for completion in 2009.

As part of DWTC's redevelopment, a second project, Exhibition City, will be constructed at Dubai World Central airport near Jebel Ali to handle the ever-expanding exhibitions industry. In addition to its exhibition areas, Exhibition City will feature hotels, offices and services related to the exhibition industry.

Some may wonder why DWTC has simultaneously launched two massive expansion projects in two different areas of Dubai but the answer is quite simple. Exhibition City will focus on exhibitions while the DWTC complex adjacent to Sheikh Zayed Road will focus on conventions.

The first phase of Exhibition City is targeted for completion in July 2009 while the first phase of the development at DWTC will be towards the end of the same year. The completion of the projects will be market driven, on the basis of incremental development. The expansion at DWTC will dramatically increase the number of MICE visitors to Dubai, while Exhibition City will double the number of exhibitions being held in the emirate. In standards it will be the best in the world; in space it will be the fourth largest behind Beijing, Milan and Hanover. On a regional basis the intention is to have the biggest convention centre and the biggest exhibition centre.

The projects will meet the needs of Dubai's mushrooming MICE sector, which currently accounts for 18 per cent of Dubai's US$30 billion GDP and comprises 40 per cent of Dubai's tourism industry.

Exhibition organizer and host

Hosting more than 70 events annually, the DICEC is one of two exhibition facilities managed by DWTC, the other being Airport Expo Dubai. This facility boasts 23,000 square metres of exhibition space in two spacious halls complemented by an expansive outdoor display area; it is home to the biennial Dubai Air Show, one of the foremost events of its type.

Several of the annual international exhibitions housed in the two complexes are organized by the DWTC Exhibition team, including the Middle East's largest and most successful information-technology exhibition, GITEX, and its retail component, Computer Shopper; while another notable exhibition is the Arabian Travel Market. International exhibitions are also staged by independent organizers; these exhibitions, together with those of the DWTC, attract hundreds of thousands of business visitors to Dubai every year.

In addition to hosting a wide range of exhibitions, DICEC and Airport Expo Dubai are a hive of activity during the annual Dubai Shopping Festival and Dubai Summer Surprises – two key promotional campaigns spearheaded by the Government of Dubai.

The Dubai Chamber of Commerce & Industry

The Dubai Chamber of Commerce & Industry (DCCI) is one of the pioneering

The biennial Dubai Air Show, held at Airport Expo Dubai, is one of the foremost events of its type, with both indoor and outdoor display areas and spectacular flight displays.

The Dubai Chamber of Commerce & Industry (building on the right), one of the pioneering chambers in the GCC, was established in 1965.

chambers in the GCC, having started operations more than 40 years ago, before the founding of the UAE. With its headquarters in an eye-catching, triangular-shaped building overlooking the Creek, the chamber has the reputation of a first-class organization that makes a major contribution to facilitating commerce in the city.

As well as being a focal point for local business, DCCI is an essential point of contact for foreign companies wishing to trade with Dubai. Its activities include arranging visits for business delegations from around the world, as well as trade missions from nearby Gulf states. Through the years the chamber has been responsible for putting many overseas exporters in touch with import houses in Dubai and promoting growth in re-exports. The chamber has close links with associated organizations involved with trade promotion in countries worldwide.

In addition to the more obvious aspects of the promoting and coordinating the growth of commerce, trade and industry in Dubai, DCCI organizes the Mohammed bin Rashid Al Maktoum Business Awards to honour the success of firms that have contributed to the UAE's economic development. DCCI also launched the annual 'Dubai the City that Cares' campaign during Ramadan in 1998. The main objectives of the campaign are to create an awareness of the needy and motivate the retail sector and the public to contribute to local charities while inspiring the youth to take up voluntary charity work. One of the earliest initiatives of DCCI, the Dubai University College, aims at assisting local businesses in administrative and vocational training. Two other important DCCI initiatives are the Dubai International Arbitration Centre and the Dubai Ethics Resource Centre.

Dubai Internet City

Dubai's development in the past few decades has been characterized by economic transformations inspired by its forward-thinking leaders and it was Sheikh Mohammed who conceived a dynamic project to transform the region into a knowledge-based economy. One of the lynch pins of this strategy was Dubai Internet City. Dubai Internet City was established with the mission of creating an infrastructure and environment for knowledge-economy companies to operate locally, regionally and globally out of Dubai and to enjoy significant advantages while doing so.

It is fully supported by the Government of Dubai and operates as a free zone that empowers companies in the community and helps them innovate and grow. It offers a unique infrastructure in modern, fully serviced offices, planned and built by leading global IT companies and based on cutting-edge technologies.

The community offers a rich network that companies can tap for resources, partnerships and ideas. Companies in Dubai Internet City not only compete with but also complement each other. The evolving community offers a high quality of business interaction and the presence of companies from across the IT spectrum creates a large pool of skills, expertise and resources.

Since its opening in 2000, Dubai Internet City has grown rapidly into a vibrant international community of companies. Several global IT giants are already part of its population: Microsoft, Oracle, HP, IBM and Canon, to name just a few. Today Dubai Internet City houses more than 850 registered companies. It's also home to more than 5,500 IT workers.

Dubai Internet City, one of the emirate's many freezones, houses more than 850 IT companies and 5,500 workers. It opened in 2000.

Dubai Media City

Similar in concept to Dubai Internet City and located adjacent to it on Sheikh Zayed Road, Dubai Media City was opened in 2001 as part of a mission to develop Dubai into a global media hub, by creating an 'infrastructure, environment and attitude' that enables media-focused enterprises to operate locally, regionally and globally with significant advantages.

It's the place where all kinds of media business – broadcasting, publishing, communication services, research, music and post-production – can thrive, and offers an advanced free-zone infrastructure that's based on state-of-the-art information and communication technologies. Since its launch, Dubai Media City has grown into a bustling media community of more than 1,000 companies and some 200 freelance professionals. Several global media giants and promising entrepreneurial ventures, including CNN, Reuters, Sony Broadcast and pan-Arabic broadcaster MBC, have joined the community.

The presence of companies from across the media-industry spectrum has created a large and useful pool of skills, expertise and resources that companies can tap into. In addition, as part of its mission of promoting talent and entrepreneurship in the region, Dubai Media City has started the Media Business Centre, a unique facility for freelance and independent media professionals.

Dubai Media City is also constantly exploring ways to ensure local media companies have the benefit of a steady supply of talent. A new Media Academy with flexible programmes has been established to train media professionals, while the annual Ibda'a Media Student Awards identify and foster young talent by providing winners internships with seasoned professionals.

To provide more space for a more diverse media community, Dubai Media City is expanding its infrastructure. Commercial, residential, educational, medical and recreational facilities are part of the attraction for media professionals and they promote an excellent quality of life in this community. Shared business centres, customer-service centres, IT services, cafes, restaurants and retail stores are all part of Dubai Media City's amenities.

Promoting Dubai

Dubai Government's Department of Tourism and Commerce Marketing (DTCM), established in 1997, has two main areas of responsibility, the first of which is to concentrate on the international promotion of Dubai's commerce and tourism interests. DTCM is also the principal authority for planning, supervising and developing tourism in the emirate.

In its marketing role, DTCM plans and implements an integrated programme of international promotions and publicity activities, including exhibition participation, marketing visits, presentations and road shows, familiarization and assisted visits, publishing books and handbooks, brochure production and distribution, media relations and enquiry-information services. In addition to its head office in Dubai, DTCM has 14 overseas offices. The department's administrative responsibilities in Dubai include the licensing of hotels, tour operators, tourist-transport companies and travel agents. Its supervisory role also covers all tourism conferences and exhibitions, the operation of tourist-information services and the organization and licensing of tour guides. It also offers a wide variety of training options for the tourism industry, and operates and manages the dedicated cruise-liner terminal that opened at Port Rashid in Dubai in 2001.

Chapter Four
Banking and Finance

To appreciate the dynamic nature and scale of the recent development of Dubai's financial community, a quick look at recent history will help put it into perspective. The first bank established in Dubai was HSBC, in 1946, although at the time it bore the impressive name of the Imperial Bank of Persia. The introduction helped revolutionize trade in the emirate.

Twenty years later, Dubai reached a historic turning point when oil was discovered offshore. During the 1970s the whole of the Gulf region, including Dubai, experienced growth of unprecedented proportions. For the banks this meant huge business, both to service a construction boom and to finance the expansion of trade as imports surged.

Many of the well-established local banking names were set up at this time, in the late 1960s and early 1970s, largely to cope with the extra cash flows generated by the new oil wealth. The National Bank of Dubai was formed in 1963 by Sheikh Rashid and a group of local businessmen and was swiftly followed by the development of several family-based banks, including the Bank of Oman, the Middle East Bank and the Union Bank of the Middle East. There were also banks with more widely based shareholdings, such as the Commercial Bank of Dubai and the Dubai Islamic Bank, founded in 1975.

At the same time, various foreign banks obtained licences to operate in what is

The Gate was the first building completed in the Dubai International Financial Centre and represents a gateway for capital and investment into the region.

The healthy competition between Dubai's various banks extends to state-of-the-art automated teller machines.

now the UAE, led by Citibank in 1964. By the late 1970s, it had become obvious that, with the number at around 50, there were just too many banks in the UAE to serve a population of 1.5 million since this equated to one financial institution for every 30,000 people. Such over-banking resulted in heavy competition, which in turn resulted in lower margins, with fewer funds being available for reserves.

This untenable position was tackled by the Central Bank of the UAE, which was founded in its present form in 1980 and actively encouraged mergers between local banks. But it was the oil-price drop in the early 1980s that finally led to a shake-up of the UAE banking community.

By 1988, the number of commercial banks in the UAE (now with a much larger population) stood at 47, with 19 of them local; there were 286 bank branches and six Dubai-based banks.

Although the consolidation of banking into larger units was – and still is – a worldwide phenomenon, all of Dubai's banks look forward to the future with confidence founded on a very successful history and are diversifying their products and services to be more competitive in the local market. They have upgraded their retail banking operations with services such as state-of-the-art automated teller machines (ATMs) for personal banking, sophisticated credit cards, highly competitive personal loans and online banking solutions. On the other hand – the commercial one – many banks have geared up for the globalization of the UAE financial sector.

Indeed, the year 2005 was a boom year for banks in the UAE and Dubai and the country's banking sector recorded an incredible performance with net profits increasing by an exceptional 120 per cent to US$4.3 billion (Dhs 15.8 billion). Many banks reported net profit increases well in excess of 100 per cent and strong growth was seen in assets and loans. Higher personal loans, corporate lending and trade finance resulted in a strong credit growth.

UAE banks have also recently focussed on increasing their non-interest revenues. Growing trade-finance activities have improved commissions and foreign exchange, while rising consumer banking activities have increased fee income. Investment banking income was also very strong in 2005 and Dubai banks reaped huge windfalls from IPO activity (ie initial public offering: the first issue of a company's shares to the public, used as a means of raising start-up or

expansion capital) during the year.

This strong earning trend continued in the first quarter of 2006 but results for the rest of the year indicated lower profits for a number of banks. This was attributed to less IPO activity and a fall in the stock markets in the UAE and other major exchanges in the Gulf, with the Dubai Financial Market Index falling by more than 50 per cent in the first half of 2006. Nevertheless, both the UAE's and Dubai's economy remains strong thanks to the country's oil reserves together with growth in other key areas such as real estate, trading and tourism and leisure.

Today, most Dubai banks are pursuing strategies that involve increasing retail and consumer banking assets and associated products, while maintaining existing corporate business. Investment banking, private banking for high-net-worth individuals, and asset management are also becoming increasingly important for most Dubai banks. Competition is tough, and getting tougher in a small market where some 50 banks, domestic and foreign, compete for business.

As in other GCC markets, Islamic banking and finance is also growing rapidly. A number of Dubai banks are pursuing Islamic assets while others have expanded their Islamic-finance operations. The Dubai Islamic Bank is one of the two main Islamic banking institutions in the country and is growing swiftly, investing in technology and expanding its distribution channels, product range and the concept of women-only branches. Other Islamic financial institutions in Dubai, such as the mortgage house, Amlak, are also showing impressive growth.

The establishment of the Dubai International and Financial Centre (DIFC) has

A number of Dubai banks are pursuing Islamic assets while others have expanded their Islamic finance operations.

Dubai banks are pursuing strategies that involve increasing retail and consumer banking assets and associated products, while maintaining existing corporate business.

also benefited the banking sector in Dubai by providing wider opportunities for income diversity, particularly with regard to earnings streams such as asset management, investment banking and corporate finance.

Dubai contributes roughly a quarter of the country's GDP but this includes a substantial portion of non-oil sector activity. Adapting the best practices from round the globe, the emirate has become the regional business base and headquarters for a number of leading international banks. With some of the national banks already having balance sheets that would be the envy of any bank in the world, impressive liquidity ratios and excellent profit records, Dubai is fast establishing itself as an important market for the international banking industry.

Dubai Financial Market

Located in the Dubai World Trade Centre, the Dubai Financial Market (DFM) was established to create a fair, efficient and transparent marketplace that serves the interests of the national economy while providing investors with opportunities to invest their funds to best advantage. The DFM constantly seeks to accomplish these objectives while protecting the investments and savings of investors, in general, and small investors in particular. It's equipped with state-of-the-art systems and technology to provide maximum liquidity in securities trading. The DFM operates on an automated screen-based trading system – similar to those which most of the world's major stock exchanges have upgraded to in recent years – which offers a distinct advantage over traditional floor trading.

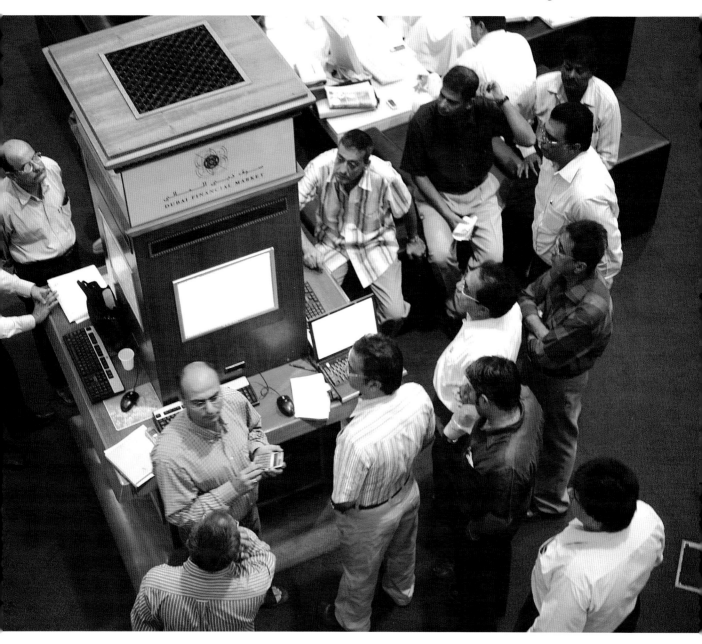

Only accredited brokers are allowed to deal in securities listed at the DFM and the broker's selection and accreditation process is rigorous. All DFM-accredited brokers have offices on the trading floor, where they're provided with workstations and means to communicate with their clients and carry out orders efficiently.

The trading floor is open to investors during operating hours and provides facilities such as large screens displaying real-time trading data. Additional space is available in the visitors' gallery, overlooking the trading floor, which contains computer terminals that can be used by investors to view details and outstanding buy-and-sell orders.

The DFM was established as a step to complete the institutional framework of the financial sector and to further consolidate the UAE's position as a regional and international financial centre. Striving to become the unique investment destination for all local and international investment, DFM satisfies all market categories by providing unique services and an extraordinary trading environment.

The DFM operates on an automated, screen-based trading system – similar to the one used in most of the world's major stock exchanges. Only brokers are allowed to deal in securities.

Dubai International Financial Centre

The Dubai International Financial Centre (DIFC), launched in 2002, was a calculated move in Dubai's grand strategy to diversify from oil and become the regional hub for finance, tourism, trade, IT and services. With the launch of DIFC, Dubai has come one step closer to being the financial powerhouse of the region – just as Hong Kong and Singapore are in the Far East.

DIFC focuses on various sectors of financial activity: banking services, capital markets, asset management and fund registration, insurance and reinsurance, Islamic finance, business-processing operations and ancillary services. Financial institutions may apply for licences in the above sectors, which are issued by the Dubai Financial Services Authority (DFSA). A part of DIFC, the authority regulates financial services in the DIFC to international standards and creates a legal framework within which to operate.

The Dubai International Financial Exchange or DIFX, a complementary body to DIFC that created the Emirates' first stock exchange, was established in 2005 in an effort to complete the global financial system, essentially filling a gap not yet covered by the international financial centres of Europe, the Far East and North America.

In celebration of its one-year anniversary, the DIFC opened The Gate, an iconic building representing a gateway for capital and investment into the region. This shouldn't prove too difficult with the impressive list of financial giants DIFC is amassing, including international heavyweights such as Mellon Financial Corporation, global financial-services firm Morgan Stanley, the renowned accounting firm of PricewaterhouseCoopers and the investment-banking firm, Jefferies International Limited. In addition, DIFC also attracts other finance-related businesses such as credit-rating agencies, professional service firms, law firms and information service providers.

Located in a prime area parallel to Sheikh Zayed Road and adjacent to Jumeirah Emirates Towers, DIFC is bound to give impetus to the banking and financial performance of the region as it 'aims to cooperate further with the IMF in providing better understanding of the region's economies and financial markets and promoting their development'. The establishment of DIFC has benefited the banking sector, providing wider opportunities for income diversity, particularly in regard to asset management, investment banking and corporate finance.

Business Bay

Aimed at making Dubai a global and commercial business centre, the multi-billion-dollar Business Bay is being created as a commercial and business district, similar to New York's Manhattan and Toyko's Ginza business centres. It will provide a conducive environment and sound infrastructure for businesses from round the world and will be built along an extension of Dubai Creek, stretching from Ra's al-Khor to Sheikh Zayed Road.

Business Bay will feature office and residential towers in landscaped gardens interspersed with a network of roads, pathways and canals. The ambitious project will provide a highly conducive environment and infrastructure for businesses from around the world to establish their regional and international headquarters.

Business Bay has a solid backing. It is being developed by Dubai Properties, a member of government-owned Dubai Holding, which is also developing Culture Village alongside Dubai Creek; Jumeirah Beach Residence, described as 'the largest single-phase residential and commercial project in the world'; and The Villa, 'the region's largest and most comprehensive leisure, tourism, entertainment and lifestyle complex at Dubailand'.

Until recently, the iconic Jumeirah Emirates Towers, in the heart of Dubai's financial district, was the tallest building in Europe and the Middle East. It has now been eclipsed by Burj Dubai.

Chapter Five
Real Estate

Dubai is enjoying a property boom with new developments such as apartments, villas and offices, springing up all over the emirate.

Attractive new residential areas have transformed the face of Dubai, changing arid desert into vibrant communities with comfortable lifestyles.

In 2002, freehold ownership for nationals as well as expatriates in certain select property developments was introduced in Dubai and 25-year mortgage loans became available. This move initiated a property boom and a concept that was quickly copied by other emirates and the Gulf states.

In the beginning, focus was centred on The Palm and other prestigious developments of the Nakheel and Emaar property companies. More companies soon became involved and the developments expanded to include freehold office accommodation. In less than a handful of years, the industry has become a classic example of the way in which Dubai's influence and expertise is expanding internationally – an important component of Dubai's vision for the future.

Most of these new developments were designed and developed for a convenient lifestyle and a sense of community, with their own international schools, shopping centres, community centres, sport and leisure facilities, medical facilities, health clubs, parks, restaurants, hotels, maintenance services and 24-hour security.

Not surprisingly, homeowners who'd invested in property in Dubai saw the values of their villas and apartments increase rapidly with the property boom. By the end of 2006, some people felt a levelling could be expected in line with an oversupply of housing; others felt that Dubai's increasing population and the investment market would keep the real-estate market buoyant and that Dubai properties still offered great value when compared with the cost of housing elsewhere.

However, it also needs to be borne in mind that the GCC plans to introduce a monetary union in 2010 and that economists expect the dirham to be upwardly revalued alongside fellow Gulf currencies (such as the Saudi riyal) against the US dollar. At present the dirham is artificially undervalued and this contributes to high inflation and low interest rates. A unified GCC currency with its own central bank would set an interest rate and currency value more in line with local circumstances with the result that property investments in the GCC would increase in terms of foreign currencies although mortgage rates would also be higher.

Nakheel

The Palm has been described as the 'Eighth Wonder of the World' and is the sort of project that some say could only have taken place in Dubai. The Palm consists of three large, man-made islands: The Palm Jumeirah, The Palm Jebel Ali and The Palm Deira. Each island is being built by the developers, Nakheel, in the shape of a palm tree, consisting of a crown of between 17 and 41 fronds, a trunk and a surrounding 'Crescent Island', the back of which forms a protective breakwater. At least 85-million cubic metres of rock and sand will be needed to build each island, of which the smallest, The Palm Jumeirah, is six-kilometres long and 5.5-kilometres wide.

Approximately 3,000 homes and at least 40 luxury hotels will be built on The Palm Jumeirah and The Palm Jebel Ali. There'll also be four marinas (two on each island) capable of berthing a total of 400 yachts.

The Palm Jumeirah is the project that started it all and doubled Dubai's original shoreline. Planned as a quiet residential retreat and a destination of world-class hotels, anchored by The Palm Trump International Hotel & Tower, the island was built off the Jumeirah coastline, opposite Dubai Internet City and about 25 kilometres from the centre of Dubai.

The second island in The Palm family, The Palm Jebel Ali, was designed as a getaway for residents and visitors alike, with an array of luxury hotels, waterhomes

Two of Dubai's island developments taking shape off Jumeirah: The Palm Jumeirah (left) and The World.

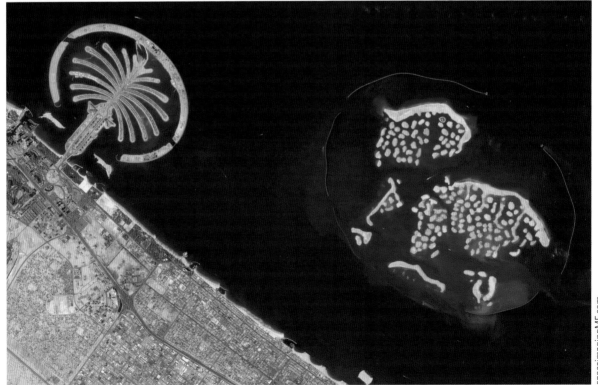

spaceimagingME.com

built on stilts, beachside villas, shoreline apartments, dive sites and a variety of entertainment and leisure activities. The island is being built 15 kilometres from The Palm Jumeirah, just south-west of Jebel Ali port and 10 kilometres from the Abu Dhabi border.

The final chapter in The Palm trilogy, The Palm Deira, will further enhance the value of Deira by unlocking access to waterfront communities that will be developed on the man-made island.

Another iconic and much talked about island project of Nakheel's is The World, 300 man-made islands in the shape of the world, located off the coast of Dubai, that are available for leisure, residential or tourist developments. Adding more than 232 kilometres of new beachfront to Dubai's coastline, The World offers islands ranging from 14,000 square metres to 42,000 square metres in size, and will be accessible by marine or air transport, with world-class marinas servicing the development.

Dubai Waterfront, adjacent to The Palm Jebel Ali, is claimed to be the largest waterfront development in the world and will be bigger than Manhattan and Beirut, offering investors more than 250 planned areas. The vision behind Dubai Waterfront is to create a world-class destination for residents, visitors and businesses in the world's fastest growing city.

At the time of publication, Nakheel had 15 major projects worth more than Dhs 110 billion (US$30 billion) under development. Once complete, these developments will add more than 1,500 kilometres of beachfront to the Dubai coastline, and will spread across more than 30,000 hectares of the city. The developments include six residential communities:

Discovery Gardens is located in Jebel Ali, next to Nakheel's Ibn Battuta Mall, and consists of more than 26,000 apartments of various sizes.

The Gardens is a family-oriented neighbourhood next to Jebel Ali Village. Like Discovery Gardens, it is close to the Ibn Battuta Mall. The first phase was completed in 2003 and is home to 10,000 residents.

Jumeirah Golf Estates brings Nakheel together with golfers Greg Norman and Vijay Singh to create a residential golfing community. Comprising four eco-

Property companies such as Emaar and Nakheel are transforming large tracks of sandy desert into vibrant communities.

Dubai's International City combines residential and commercial elements. Its Dragon Mart retail complex is the largest one for Chinese products outside mainland China.

courses, Fire, Earth, Water and Wind, this distinctive community also features abundant parkland, lakes and ponds.

Jumeirah Islands is a waterfront community in the heart of the desert; a 300-hectare residential development created with families in mind. Here, an array of homes is surrounded by lush landscaping, winding canals, waterfalls and lagoons.

Jumeirah Village encompasses more than 6,000 villas and townhouses, adjacent to Jumeirah Islands and accessed by Al Khail Road.

The Lost City is a residential development inspired by famous cities in Arabian history and combines this with the best of modern amenities. The development will be located in Jebel Ali, adjacent to Nakheel's other developments, Ibn Battuta Shopping Mall and Discovery Gardens.

Two other residential communities being developed by Nakheel form part of wider-ranging projects that are also a home to various commercial activities:

The Arabian Canal is set to transform Dubai by 'integrating the sea and the desert', turning barren areas into numerous communities, districts and neighbourhoods, encompassing a diverse mix of entertainment, retail, commercial, hospitality and residential developments. The focal point of this massive engineering project will be an 80-kilometre canal that will provide a new transportation network for recreational and commercial use in Dubai.

International City combines commercial, residential, retail and tourism elements from different parts of the world. In all, the project has five districts including the Central Business District, Residential District, the Lake District around Al Warsan Lake, the Dragon Mart complex (the largest retail complex for Chinese products outside mainland China), and Forbidden City (a replica of the Forbidden City in China) which hosts a variety of entertainment facilities.

Completing Nakheel's Dubai portfolio at the time of going to press were two purely commercial projects:

Dubai Design Centre, a centre for traders and retailers, which offers a complete range of home furnishing, design, gardening and construction options.

Ibn Battuta Mall, the largest single-floor shopping mall in the world, is themed around the travels of the Arabian explorer, Ibn Battuta. The architecture within the mall's six courts reflects the most influential places Ibn Battuta travelled to.

Nakheel Hotels & Resorts, a new hotel and resort investment company, was launched early in 2006 to oversee the development of hotels, such as the Trump International Hotel & Tower on The Palm Jumeirah, in the UAE, as well as the development and acquistion of hotels and resorts internationally, commencing in Russia, the Middle East, Africa and Asia.

Arabian Ranches is a pleasant residential development typical of Dubai and features an equestrian centre, a polo ground and an attractive desert golf course.

Emaar Properties

Emaar Properties, one of the largest property developers in the Middle East, was established in Dubai in 1997. It is jointly owned by the Government of Dubai and individual investors, through a listing on the Dubai Financial Market. The company has witnessed tremendous growth since its inception in 1997.

Emaar Properties is developing world-class projects that are helping to transform the architectural face of the region – using designs that pay homage to Arabian roots, while enhancing the reputation of Dubai and the UAE as a thriving centre for economic growth and technological advancement.

Currently, Emaar has several major real estate projects completed or under development in Dubai, including Dubai Marina, Emirates Hills, The Meadows, The Springs, Arabian Ranches, The Greens, The Views and The Lakes among others. The company also owns and manages the Gold and Diamond Park.

Dubai Marina will eventually boast more than 200 apartment towers, office blocks, hotels, luxury villas and berthing for yachts and leisure craft. The sport facilities include marine clubs and one of the amenities is Marina Walk, a promenade of fine-dining restaurants, coffee shops, a supermarket and retail outlets.

Emirates Hills is a desirable community of well-appointed villas with a Middle Eastern flavour, surrounded by tranquil scenery, lakes and the Montgomerie golf course. The complex has a restricted-access policy with round-the-clock security and maintenance. It also offers some of the largest plots in Dubai.

The Meadows is a large area of tree-lined streets and spacious double-storey villas located next to Emirates Hills. These homes range from three to seven bedrooms in size and the neighbourhood has swimming pools, landscaped parks, lakes, children's play areas and 24-hour security.

The Springs is a gated community of Arabian-styled town houses within Emirates Hills. The scenic waterways and lush landscaping tend to attract young families and couples. The Springs shares international schools, nurseries, health clubs, three shopping centres, restaurants and mosques with Emirates Hills and The Meadows, and is close to both the Montgomerie and Emirates Golf Club.

Arabian Ranches, set within the 'heart of the desert', is a residential development featuring an equestrian centre and polo ground and a golf course designed by Peter Baker-Finch in association with Nicklaus Design, and 3,850 residential units.

The Greens consists of a number of apartment blocks, with each apartment set in one of four buildings positioned to enclose a private courtyard for all residents to enjoy. Each complex has a gym and shared barbecue facilities and there is secure underground parking and state-of-the-art security. The Greens is situated next to Emirates Golf Club and is close to Dubai Media and Internet Cities, Dubai Marina, American University of Dubai and Sheikh Zayed Road.

The Views is located adjacent to The Greens. Overlooking waterways and the Emirates Golf Club, it is a 'vibrant community' of townhouses and apartments that offers swimming pools and decks, barbeque areas, gymnasiums, mini sports courts, play areas, parks, underground and covered parking.

The Lakes provides homes from two to five bedrooms for rent and sale in a tranquil neighbourhood featuring waterways, parks and landscaped greenery. There's also a popular community centre, bicycle pathways and 24-hour maintenance and security. Its villas are situated between two world-class golf courses, The Montgomerie at Emirates Hills and Emirates Golf Club.

Emaar's latest and most anticipated development is **Burj Dubai**, an iconic superstructure which, when complete in 2009, will be the tallest building in the world and a global tourist magnet. The Burj Dubai neighbourhood will also house one of the largest shopping malls in the world, Dubai Mall; while The Old Town will feature intimate streets and architectural detail with the special ambience and mystery of old Arabia. Typically for Dubai, there will also be man-made lakes and waterways, landscaped parks and gardens.

In line with its – and Dubai's – international expansion strategy, Emaar has joint ventures and projects across the region, covering the Middle East and North Africa (MENA) and the Indian subcontinent, including Egypt, Turkey, Syria, Saudi Arabia, Morocco, Tunisia, India and Pakistan.

Emaar is aggressively diversifying from property development into retail, leisure, hospitality, health, education and finance with the mission of becoming one of the world's most valuable companies in less than five years. It plans to develop approximately 100 shopping malls in the emerging markets of the MENA region and the Indian subcontinent.

In addition, Emaar has teamed up with Giorgio Armani SpA to build and manage 10 Armani hotels and resorts across the world, including one in Emaar's flagship Burj Dubai tower. The education initiative will involve the establishment of international schools in the MENA region and India, while Emaar plans to enter the healthcare sector in the MENA and South Asian markets with the construction of 100 hospitals, clinics and medical centres.

Emaar also owns and manages Emrill, which provides property management services, holds a 30-per-cent equity in Dubai Bank and is the majority shareholder in Amlak Finance, an Islamic home-financing company.

When complete, Dubai Marina will boast more than 200 apartment towers, office blocks, hotels, luxury villas, restaurants and berthing for leisure craft.

Dubailand

Part of government-owned Dubai Holding, Dubailand is a tourism, entertainment, and leisure complex of enormous magnitude. Phase one of the project is expected to be completed in 2008, while a few of the attractions, such as the Dubai Autodrome and The Global Village are already operational.

The development is divided into six themes or 'worlds' and the short-range goal of the Dubailand is to attract 15-million tourists to Dubai by 2010. The developers expect to accomplish this by creating a destination that will attract visitors not only from surrounding countries but also from Europe and Asia.

In the longer term, Dubailand is seen as one of the ways to phase out Dubai's dependence on oil revenues. When complete, the venture is expected to attract approximately 200,000 visitors daily and cost more than Dhs 70 billion (US$20 billion). It will be twice the size of Walt Disney World Resort in Florida, currently the largest collection of amusement parks in the world.

Completion of the fourth and final phase is targeted for some time between 2015 and 2018 but Dubailand is seen by its designers as a city and, like a city, they expect it to continue to grow and develop beyond the four-phase plan. The six theme worlds will be:

Attractions and Experience World, the anchor attraction of Dubailand, which will include theme parks, water parks, roller coasters, The Global Village, Kid's City and Giants' World.

Retail and Entertainment World incorporating a flea market, World Trade Park, Auction World and factory outlets.

Leisure and Vacation World has been designed to respond to the growing international demand for quality vacation village residences, resort hotels and wellness retreats. This will be home to the Andalusian Resort & Spa, The Indian Theme Resort, Women's World, The Nubian Village, The Silver Street Resort and the Thai Express Resort.

Ecotourism World will comprise a series of nature and desert-based attractions, including Al Barari, Dubai Heritage Village, Life World, Pet Land, Safari Park, Sand Dune Hotel and Tropical Village Desert Safari.

Sports and Outdoor World will be home to Dubai Sports City, Emarat Sports World, Plantation Equestrian and Polo Club, Dubai Autodrome, Dubai Golf City, Extreme Sports World and Golf World. A mix of sporting venues will incorporate a dynamic program of international rugby, cricket and other sports tournaments as well as extreme sports activities.

Downtown, Retail and Entertainment World will provide a mix of entertainment, shopping and eating out. It will provide popular family entertainment and will contain five main attractions: City of Arabia, incorporating the Mall of Arabia which (together with Burj Dubai's Dubai Mall) will be the world's largest shopping mall, Dubai Bazaar, Dubai Outlet City, a restaurant complex, Teen World and Virtual Games World.

Dubailand will be conveniently located along Emirates Road and the Dubai–Al Ain Road, providing easy access from Abu Dhabi, Al Ain, Dubai and Sharjah.

Jumeirah Beach Residence

Jumeirah Beach Residence is comprised of 36 luxury apartment towers and four hotel towers. It is located on the north shore of the Dubai Marina, close to the Palm Jumeirah and is designed to offer a beach-resort lifestyle to its residents while catering to people and families of different nationalities, with varying budgets and needs.

Jumeirah Beach Residence will be home to more than 25,000 residents and will be a self-contained community with amenities such as restaurants, cinemas,

health clubs, sport centres, medical facilities, beach clubs, children's play areas, housekeeping, retail stores, supermarkets, nursery schools and more.

The project is being developed by the same team that developed Dubai Internet City, Dubai Media City and Knowledge Village.

The Lagoons

In 2006, Sama Dubai, a private company wholly owned by Dubai Holding, launched its new waterfront project, The Lagoons, which is being built alongside Dubai Creek. The total project cost is estimated at Dhs 65 billion (US$18 billion) and the development will be spread across an area of 6.5 million square metres. Half of the project will be sold to third-party investors as plots for development, while the remaining 50 per cent of the area will be developed, marketed and operated by Sama Dubai.

The project will consist of seven landscaped islands interlinked with bridges and comprising residential units, shopping centres, office buildings and marinas. The project will also incorporate a unique work environment with its own CBD where multi-nationals and regional corporations can establish their headquarters.

The Lagoons is one of the first projects in Dubai to undertake a comprehensive Integrated Environmental Impact Assessment (EIA) following international standards across all phases of the project. Sama Dubai is working in cooperation with Dubai Municipality to explore ways to protect and enhance the wildlife sanctuary in Ra's al-Khor so as to ensure The Lagoons and the sanctuary are symbiotic neighbours.

The project will incorporate themes of environment, conservation, parkland and open spaces, and will include resorts, five-star hotels, commercial towers, high-end villas and uptown apartments. The Lagoons will also boast Dubai's first opera house and other planned cultural elements include a planetarium, museum, art centre and theatre.

Global Village, part of Dubailand and Experience World, is already fully operational and attracts thousands of visitors during the Dubai Shopping Festival.

Property companies in Dubai have transformed the desert into desirable residential communities and these have been enhanced by the gardens created by residents.

The private sector

Increasingly, private companies are becoming involved in Dubai's property industry, and one of the first developers to make a major commitment was Damac Properties. Today, Damac is not only considered as one of the largest but as a market leader, with a strong sales record to its credit.

Damac is one of the UAE's leading providers of waterfront luxury projects, as well as the name behind some acclaimed residential and commercial developments in Dubai. Some of its notable projects are situated in Dubai Marina, Palm Island Jumeirah, Palm Island Jebel Ali, Jumeirah Lakes Towers, Dubailand and Dubai International Financial Centre.

The total value of Damac's projects is more than Dhs 15 billion (US$4 billion) and Damac Holding has now grown into a global conglomerate with more than 6,000 employees in 18 countries.

Chapter Six
Industry

Before the coming of federation, Dubai broke with the strategy adopted by many of its neighbours in the Gulf by deciding not to base its economic dependence on oil reserves that would one day run out. Headed by its ruler, Sheikh Rashid, the emirate adopted earnest and far-sighted measures to ensure diversification into other industries.

Today, through sheer determination, hard work and substantial investment from Dubai's government, it's clear that this decision has taken the emirate along the path to commercial success. Dubai has developed into the fastest-growing and most attractive business centre in the Middle East.

Although Abu Dhabi has far greater oil reserves, Dubai is the second-largest producer of oil in the UAE. The majority of its crude-oil production comes from four offshore fields: Fateh, SW Fateh, Falah and Rashid, operated by the Dubai Petroleum Company.

In addition to oil, Dubai produces a substantial quantity of gas. The end product, in the form of liquid butane and propane, is sold commercially, both locally and internationally. Other petroleum by-products are used by the Dubai

After the oil industry, the Dubai Aluminium Company is the UAE's industrial flagship. It celebrated its 25th anniversary in 2004.

49

Dubal is situated adjacent to Jebel Ali Port, close to the Dubai–Abu Dhabi highway. The company is on the way to becoming the largest aluminium producer in the world.

Aluminium Company (DUBAL) and the Dubai Electricity and Water Authority (DEWA). The Dubai Natural Gas Company (DUGAS) is another user of the extensive gas supply, mainly from the offshore fields. The onshore Margham gas field is operated by the Atlantic Richfield Company.

Dubai Aluminium Company

After the oil industry, Dubal is the UAE's industrial flagship. The company's operations, based on a 480-hectare site, 35 kilometres from the centre of Dubai, include an aluminium smelter, a power station and a desalination plant capable of producing 136 million litres of fresh water every day.

Dubal employs more than 3,200 skilled professionals, craftsmen, support staff and operators, nearly a fifth of whom are UAE nationals in positions of increasing responsibility. Its location in Dubai facilitates the company's ability to source raw materials and gives it a competitive advantage in key markets around the world. Excellent port facilities enable it to receive high-quality raw materials from its suppliers and to expedite shipments to markets in Japan, Korea, Taiwan, China, Thailand, Indonesia, Malaysia, Singapore, the United States and Europe.

Dubal is one of the largest suppliers of foundry alloy for the world's automotive-wheel manufacturing industry. It also produces extrusion billet for architectural purposes such as window frames, and is a top producer of high-purity aluminium used in the manufacture of compact discs and electronics components. All the aluminium produced at Dubal is of excellent quality with purity levels as high as 99.97 per cent.

A relatively young smelter by industry standards, Dubal has nevertheless achieved phenomenal success. The company has undergone several major expansion projects since its inception in 1979, making it the third-largest single-site smelter in the Western hemisphere.

Dubal presently contributes more to Dubai's GDP than oil does. Expansion projects since 1996 have resulted in more than US$2 billion (Dhs 7 billion) in investment. In 2006, Dubal sold a record 861,000 tonnes of aluminium and sales were expected to rise to 920,000 tonnes in 2008. Already the largest single-site smelter outside Russia, Dubal was well on its way to becoming the largest aluminium producer in the world.

But even this will be eclipsed by a new smelter being developed at Taweelah in Abu Dhabi by Dubal and Abu Dhabi's Mubadala Development Company. The first phase of this new smelter – a fine example of inter-emirate cooperation – is expected to be operational in 2010.

Built in the late 1970s, Dubai Drydocks, part of Port Rashid, is one of the leading ship-repair yards in the world and the largest between Europe and the Far East.

The Dubai Cable Company

Talking of inter-emirate cooperation, the Dubai Cable Company (Ducab) is the leading manufacturer of electrical cables in the Middle East. Established in 1979, the company is a joint venture between the governments of Abu Dhabi and Dubai and was one of the first 'inter-emirate' companies.

Since its inception, Ducab has grown strongly and supported the Emirates construction industry with top-quality products, helping to place the country's infrastructure on firm ground. To achieve this goal, Ducab's capacity has been expanded several times, incorporating a modern plant and technology.

Ducab has the most modern, state-of-the-art cable manufacturing and testing equipment in the Middle East. Its cable has been used in many landmark projects in Dubai, including Burj Al Arab, the Sheikh Rashid Terminal at Dubai International Airport and Jumeirah Emirates Towers. The company has always played an integral part in the industrial development of the UAE and will continue to perform a pivotal role in the region's progress.

Dubai Drydocks

Dubai Drydocks is one of the leading ship-repair yards in the world and the largest between Europe and the Far East.

Built in the late 1970s, with the aim of capitalizing on Dubai's proximity to the major oil terminals in the Arabian Gulf, Dubai Drydocks was designed to accommodate oil tankers with a capacity of up to one million tonnes of dead weight. The three huge graving docks and the floating dock, constructed by the yard itself, provide a flexibility that's second-to-none in the industry.

Augmenting the yard's core business of ship repair is conversion and ship-building. Its experience in the field of conversions has developed progressively over the years and the yard is now able to handle a variety of large-scale conversions. Ships built at Dubai Drydocks include tugs, suction dredgers, utility vessels, barges, aluminium-hulled crewboats, pontoons and even floating docks.

Dubai Drydocks holds an exemplary track record for timely delivery and is regularly frequented by the world's leading ship owners. The yard makes a substantial contribution to the local economy, providing many business opportunities for suppliers and support companies in the marine industry.

DP World

Dubai currently re-exports goods to more than 120 countries, an exchange which is seen as vital to the development of the trading community. The re-export business benefits from the successful operation of Dubai's two main ports, Port Rashid and Jebel Ali. These two ports were combined in 1991 under one adminis-

Set to grow even further, Dubai is already one of the world's foremost air-cargo centres and has emerged as the undisputed cargo hub of the Middle East.

trative body known as Dubai Ports Authority. This merger was followed by two others in 2001 and 2005 when the Ports, Customs and Free Zone Corporation merged into one organization, allowing its clients to deal with one body, DP World, rather than three. A steady expansion of facilities and specialized equipment for handling non-containerized cargo, combined with a dynamic marketing drive in newly-emerging economies around the world, continue to fuel growth in both cargo volumes and the number of shipping lines (currently totalling more than 100) using Port Rashid and Jebel Ali. This steady growth has helped consolidate the corporation's position as the largest container port operator in the the Middle East.

The Dubai Ports, offering 82 berths and 125 quayside cranes, are one of DP World's flagship facilities and were ranked ninth Top Container Port worldwide in 2005.

Dubai Cargo Village

Dubai is also one of the world's leading air-cargo centres. With the opening of the purpose-built Dubai Cargo Village in 1991, the city emerged as the cargo hub of the Middle East, serving not only the Arab World, Africa and the Indian subcontinent but, increasingly, new markets much further afield, including Europe, Asia and Australia. Located adjacent to Dubai International Airport, the Cargo Village handled more than 106,000 tonnes during a one-month period in 2006. It is therefore anticipated that Dubai Cargo Village will soon be handling more than a million tonnes annually. Increasing pressure from air-cargo users has been so great that the Cargo Village is planning to expand its facilities with the creation of a new mega cargo terminal.

Depending on actual growth, it's proposed that, by 2010, the existing cargo terminal will be demolished and replaced with the final phase of the mega terminal, offering a capacity of 2.7-million tonnes per year in addition to the 12-million-tonnes capacity expected at Dubai World Central airport. When completed it will be the most advanced air-cargo terminal in the world.

Free zones

Traditionally, a free zone is an area in a port or a city where goods may be received and held without payment of duty. In modern times in Dubai this definition has expanded somewhat and, for legal purposes, companies operating within free zones are treated as being offshore, or outside the UAE.

This has distinct advantages with regard to ownership in that companies are not required to have local partners, are free to transfer profits and capital whenever required and are exempt from corporate tax. Most free zones offer a range of business incentives that are free from red tape and restrictions, in a pleasant, modern working environment. Commerce, technology and industry have begun to complement the traditional trading base in free zones and are set to increase in importance in the near future.

The pioneer of the concept in Dubai, and one of the most successful free zones in the world, is the **Jebel Ali Free Zone Authority** (JAFZA). Since its establishment in 1985, the Jebel Ali Free Zone Authority has succeeded in attracting large and renowned companies – both on a local and an international level – which, in turn, has boosted trade and the country's economy worldwide.

Up until 1990, the number of companies situated at Jebel Ali barely exceeded 300; there are now more than 5,000 companies from 119 countries, with 15 new companies joining each month. Names such as Acer, Black & Decker, Nissan, Samsung, Sony and Xerox make up just a portion of JAFZA's profile.

Jebel Ali Free Zone has always encouraged foreign companies from various fields and specializations to establish themselves in the free zone. The policy has enhanced Jebel Ali's contribution into exports from the UAE while offering its customers a wide range of products to satisfy their needs, including but not limited to: furniture and wooden supplies, paper and paper derivatives, printing, textiles, ready-made garments, leather, food products, beverages, chemicals, petrochemical, coal, rubber, plastic, metals and machinery.

In the industrial sector, other free zones in Dubai include:

Dubai Aid City: situated in Jebel Ali Free Zone; provides international aid organizations with a hub from which to organize humanitarian efforts. www.dubaiaidcity.ae

Dubai Airport Free Zone: allows investors, especially those dealing in high-value, low-volume products, to enjoy the benefits and facilities offered by Dubai Air Cargo and Cargo Village. www.dafza.ae

Dubai Cars and Automotive Zone: managed by the Jebel Ali Free Zone Authority; facilitates the re-exporting of cars to the Asian and African region. www.ducamz.ae

Dubai Flower Centre: located at Dubai International Airport; a trans-shipment hub for flowers and perishables. www.dubaiflowercentre.com

Dubai Healthcare City: provides high quality healthcare services to the region. www.dhcc.ae

Dubai Metal and Commodities Centre: a marketplace established to bring together the gold trade, the diamond trade and other selected commodities. www.dmcc.ae

Gold and Diamond Park: owned and managed by Emaar, provides manufacturers and retailers with the opportunity to compete in international markets by offering lower operating costs. www.jafza.ae

Knowledge Village: an educational community situated close to Dubai Internet City and Dubai Media City. www.kv.ae

Forthcoming free zones in Dubai include:

Dubai Auto Parts City Free Zone: will be a centre for traders in spare parts for motor vehicles.

The Gold and Diamond Park has become more and more popular with shoppers since it opened in 2001 and was being expanded in 2007.

Dubai Knowledge Village complements Dubai Internet City and Dubai Media City by training and developing the region's talent pool.

Dubai Biotechnology and Research Park: will create an arena for international and regional scientists to conduct research, development and production.

Dubai Carpet Zone: will target the handmade carpet sector.

Dubai Maritime City: will be the world's largest maritime development and will be located on a man-made peninsula between Port Rashid and Dubai Drydocks; will encompass marine marketing, management, service, recreation, education and ship design and manufacture.

Dubai Silicon Oasis: will be a technology community housing microelectronics- and optoelectronics-related enterprises. It's set to feature fabrication plants, research and development centres, specialized academic institutions and residential areas.

Dubai Textile City: will cater to the UAE's burgeoning textile industry.

Heavy Equipment and Trucks Free Zone: will aim to boost the re-exporting of trucks and heavy equipment; will operate under the Jebel Ali Free Zone umbrella.

International Media Production Zone: will encourage major printing and publishing companies in Dubai to set up operations, with future plans including music, film and broadcasting.

Techno Park: will focus on hi-tech services, oil and gas, and desalination and water technologies while tapping the regional oil and gas, chemical, environmental and scientific research market. Environmental-management companies will focus on water-resource management, biosaline products and technology, pollution-management and control systems, and recycling industries.

Government funding

Dubai's industries have all required extensive capital investment and, in all instances, this has been provided by the government.

The planning behind government investment is meticulous. Financial support on a massive scale is provided only when the government is satisfied that the industry concerned would be a major user of labour and materials; an industry that would benefit Dubai's economy. The government insists that these industries are competitive in world markets and also produce goods to the highest standards.

There are exceptions: Emaar, one of Dubai's major property developers, in which the government has the major shareholding, and private Dubai individuals the remainder. The concept is designed to involve the private sector in heavy industry and, to date, the combination of government and private ownership is working well.

The private sector in industry

Writing in his book *My Vision – Challenges in the Race for Excellence*, Sheikh Mohammed generously credits the private sector for Dubai's achievements, stating that the government wouldn't have been able to achieve so much without its help, "Our success is that of the private sector first and then of the government."

Nevertheless, with the exception of the oil industry, the private-sector industry in Dubai must target its production into a well-recognized market or the companies will fail. Problems concerning costs of labour and imported raw materials have caused concern to certain industries such as cement production, plastics, iron and steel.

The steel industry in the UAE is small in comparison to that in neighbouring countries. There are two major players: Steelmakers Gulf Inc, based in Jebel Ali Free Zone, which is a mini steel plant producing approximately 20,000 tonnes of steel billets and rolling about 70,000 tonnes of bars and structurals annually, and the Shattaf Anand Steel Rolling Mills in Sharjah, whose three rolling mills produce 16,000 tonnes of mild steel ingots and 36,500 tonnes of deformed bars and structurals annually.

The production of plastics is highly successful thanks to a wide range of products and imports of relatively cheap raw plastic. One company, Union Plastics in Rashidiya, has developed close links with Saudi Arabia and much of its

The city of Dubai has always been a trading and re-export centre and this tradition continues today, supported strongly by the private sector.

production goes to the Saudi market or to other GCC countries.

The first bottle-production plant in the UAE, the US$50 million Al Tajer Glass Factory, has eliminated the need for imports. Full production at the Jebel Ali industrial site since March 1997 has ensured a daily output of 1.25 million bottles. It's one of the largest ever private-sector industrial investments in the UAE; a 30,000 square metre warehouse holds up to 100 days' production, and a dedicated applied-ceramic-labelling facility means that the fully automated plant can produce almost any kind of bottle.

Success or failure of cement industries depends to a great extent on the amount of construction taking place and that, of course, is tied to the strength of the economy at any one time. Dubai continues to see a great deal of development in its construction sector and this has prompted a great demand for cement. Major cement manufacturers also maintain close commercial links with other GCC countries enjoying their own building booms.

Dubai International Airport

Dubai prides itself on being a regional hub for industry, commerce and tourism – serving a surrounding population of more than 1.5 billion – while its liberal 'Open Skies' policy has attracted a large number of the world's airlines. Many of these fly dedicated services into and out of the emirate while others use Dubai as a major transit stop on their intercontinental routes. The number of airlines using Dubai has now reached 110, providing passengers with a choice of 160 destina-

Dubai International Airport is the busiest airport in the Middle East and is used by some 110 airlines serving 160 destinations.

When complete, Dubai World Central will be the largest airport in the world, with six parallel runways, each one 4.5 kilometres in length.

Emirates is the fastest growing international carrier in the world, flying to 80 destinations with new routes opening up each year.

tions, and Dubai International Airport is the busiest airport in the Middle East.

The airport has enjoyed an almost continuous history of expansion since it was first built. With the opening of the new Sheikh Rashid Terminal in 2001, it embarked on a new era. The state-of-the-art facilities and high standards of service at the terminal earned the airport the vote for best airport in the Middle East and it's well on its way to being one of the best worldwide, currently being able to handle 33-million passengers a year.

In 2005 nearly 25-million passengers used the airport and this figure is expected to touch 50 million by the end of the decade. With this in mind, the airport is undergoing yet another expansion. This includes the construction of Terminal 3, which will be devoted solely to Emirates airline, and the mega cargo terminal.

Once the second phase is completed in 2007, Dubai International Airport will be able to handle as many as 70-million passengers a year – or a staggering 190-million passengers a year when combined with Dubai World Central. This is four times the number of foreign tourists who visit America each year.

Dubai World Central International Airport

A perfect example of Dubai's bold vision is its initiative to make itself the most important aviation hub in the world. Simple in concept but massive in realization, the project will require the construction of an aviation infrastructure unmatched anywhere. When complete, Dubai World Central international airport (DWC) will be the largest airport in the world.

The colossal airport will be 10 times larger than Dubai International Airport (at least, in its 2006 guise) and Dubai Cargo Village combined, and will have a capacity equal to that of London's Heathrow and Chicago's O'Hare airports. The airport will be able to handle more than 120 million passengers and 12 million tonnes of cargo annually. Its passenger capacity will be almost 50 per cent more than Atlanta, currently the world's busiest passenger airport; while its cargo capacity will be more than three times that of Memphis, today's largest cargo hub.

Already under construction near Jebel Ali, Dubai World Central is a long-range project that will make Dubai a forerunner in passenger and air-cargo transportation, while simultaneously enhancing the emirate's capabilities as a commercial, trade and logistics hub for the Middle East and surrounding region. The plans for facilities at the Dubai World Central include:

- Six parallel runways, each four and a half kilometres in length. Up to four aircraft will be able to land simultaneously, 24 hours a day, minimizing in-air queuing.
- Designed to handle new-generation aircraft such as the Airbus A380 superjumbos ordered by Emirates airline.
- Three passenger terminals. One dedicated to aircraft of the Emirates group, the second to other carriers and the third to low-cost carriers.
- 16 Cargo terminals.
- Hotels and shopping malls.
- Support and maintenance facilities for aircraft up to A380 specifications.
- More than 100,000 parking spaces for passengers and staff.
- Linked to the Dubai International Airport by a high-speed, express rail system.

DWC will, however, be much more than an international airport. Spanning 140 square kilometres and twice the size of Hong Kong island, it will be a multi-phased development of several clustered zones advantageously positioned next to the Jebel Ali Port and Free Zone, making sea-to-air connectivity achievable in less than four hours – a world-beating turnaround time.

A self-contained city within a city, DWC's residents and workforce will exceed 750,000. It will have its own dedicated light-rail system and will be linked to the new Dubai Metro. With the latest smart technology it will be the most advanced development of its type anywhere in the world.

At the heart of this huge new community will be the international airport itself. The other components are Dubai Logistics City (a free zone to provide logistics and transportation services to the GCC, Middle East, India, Africa, South East Asia and Europe), Residential City, Commercial City, Enterprise Park and a golf resort. A seventh vital component, which is being developed and will be managed by Dubai World Trade Centre (DWTC), is Exhibition City.

Reaching for the sky

Dubai-based Emirates, the world's fastest-growing international carrier, has come a long way since it first leased a Boeing 727 in 1985. With just three flights from Dubai and a US$10 million in capital start-up, it has expanded across the world and now flies to more than 80 destinations, with new routes opening up every year.

As the fastest-growing airline in the world, Emirates has won numerous awards for everything from inflight service and entertainment to cargo operations and aircraft financing, and has one of the world's youngest fleets.

In 1992 the airline became the world's first to fit personal video screens in every seat in every class and, in 1995, the first with inflight phones and faxes. All Emirates aircraft in the future will feature the latest inflight entertainment system, called ICE (for information, communications and entertainment), with more than 500 channels, all controlled by the passenger on demand, and the airline is investing in retrofitting its existing fleet.

Movies on ICE include up to 50 of the latest releases and more than 25 all-time classic movies. For younger flyers there are 25 Disney films and there are also nearly 25 films from Arabia, Asia and the Far East.

Additionally, there are more than 50 TV channels, 40 inflight games and 350-plus audio channels, featuring more than 6,000 tracks of almost every genre imaginable, including every UK number-one hit ever. Arab customers have 13 video channels and passengers can view the latest BBC headlines, send and receive e-mail and SMS messages from any seat for just US$1 and use the telephone facility for US$5 a minute, using individual handsets.

In years to come Emirates will have two main types of aircraft, Airbus A300s and Boeing 777s, able to reach any destination in the world with only one stop. The fleet will also include A340-600s, the world's longest airliner, and a 45-strong fleet of 575-seat, double-decker Airbus A380s – including two freighters – which will be the world's largest airliners when they enter service.

With the exception of its second year, Emirates has been profitable every year it has operated. In the 12 months to April 30, 2002 and, despite the September 11 New York terror attacks, its profits rose 11 per cent, from US$115 million (Dhs 416 million) to US$127 million (Dhs 466 million) thanks to a bold 'business as usual' strategy which saw passenger numbers rise 18.3 per cent to 6.8 million. In the face of soaring fuel costs during the past few years, Emirates has still managed a staggering US$708 million (Dhs 2.6 billion) profit on operating costs of US$5.2 billion (Dhs 19 billion), carrying 12.52 million passengers in 2005 using its fleet of 90 aircraft worth a mind-boggling US$27.7 billion (Dhs 101.7 billion) – numbers that will increase when the aircraft Emirates has on order take to the skies.

As though the growth of Emirates and Dubai's colossal airports will not be enough to propel Dubai into the world's view, the emirate has also announced its intention to open the Dubai Aerospace Enterprise (DAE), a US$15 billion investment that will see the emirate capitalize on the rapidly growing air-travel sector.

Keeping in touch

Because Dubai prides itself on being a regional hub for industry and commerce, it's essential that the emirate's telecommunications capabilities grow just as quickly as its transport facilities. Since its inception in 1976, the Emirates Telecommunications Corporation, or Etisalat, has played a vital role in the development of telecommunications in the Emirates and, therefore, in establishing Dubai as one of the most advanced centres in the region and indeed the world. In 2005 there were more than four million mobile subscribers in the UAE, meaning that 95 per cent of the population, or 19 out of every 20 residents, owns a mobile phone.

The Internet continues to grow at a tremendous pace all round the world and the UAE is no exception. Established at the start of 2000, Emirates Internet and Multimedia, Etisalat's dedicated Internet unit, already has some 735,000 subscribers and an estimated 3.8 million users, the highest of any Middle Eastern country. Increased Internet bandwidth has allowed for increased usage and implementation of state-of-the-art services.

In addition to advanced communication solutions and value-added services in fixed line and GSM (a system that enables foreign visitors to use their mobile phones in the country they're visiting), Internet services and e-commerce, Etisalat's divisions and subsidiaries include Smart Cards, a data-clearing house, contact centre, submarine-cable laying and maintenance services, several international submarine cable links, an international Internet exchange, cable TV and an academy and college.

A second telecommunications company was launched in 2007. The Emirates Integrated Telecommunications Company operates under the brand name du and provides voice, data, video and content services over fixed and mobile networks to residential and corporate customers. Its offerings include voice calling, Internet, content services and television for individuals and households; integrated fixed and mobile business solutions for small and large corporations

and government agencies; as well as carrier, international data networks and wholesale services for international operators, multinational corporations and telecommunication carriers.

Throughout the UAE, Etisalat's modern tower blocks can be identified by the 'golf ball' at the top of the building.

Towards the future

Successful long-term industry in Dubai has to take into account the fundamental factors of the emirate's economy. These are: the presence of oil, the availability of inexpensive energy through gas, the availability of inexpensive labour and the possibility of substantial capital funding. However, most raw materials need to be imported and the local market is shrinking, forcing factories to look abroad for sales.

The key to success is to be able to sell at a profit, something the well-planned industries in Dubai know very well. The downstream oil industries have a naturally successful place in the world's hydrocarbon business. For example, Dugas can sell locally and abroad and has a long-term supply of raw gas.

But Dubai's future depends on its ability to consolidate its position as a commercial, industrial, financial and tourism centre of the Middle East, and to present itself to businesses across the globe as such, thereby showing itself as an attractive trading partner and offering excellent infrastructure links with some of the world's most profitable target markets.

Chapter Seven
Leisure and tourism

The Big Bus Company operates a fleet of traditional, open-top, double-decker London buses on two main routes covering the city and the beach.

Dubai has become the leading holiday destination in the Gulf and its fame has spread far and wide thanks to television travel shows, international coverage of major sporting events, and huge crowd-pullers such as the Dubai Shopping Festival and a healthy marketing budget.

Winter is especially popular with tourists; the weather is warm and sunny, the beach beckons by day and the social scene keeps the evenings busy. And the city is so safe that, when you go out in the evening, you need have no worries about wearing the gold you bought in the souk earlier in the day.

World-class facilities seem to be springing up daily, with more hotels, beach resorts and sports clubs opening their doors for business. By the end of 2006, there were 414 hotels in Dubai and 6.5 million people had stayed in them during the year, creating an average occupancy level of 85 per cent. Furthermore, a number of other hotels were under construction, including some that would be the envy of any other city in the world. This growth has been phenomenal bearing in mind that there were only 157 hotels in 1992. With a prediction of 15 million visitors by 2010, Dubai is well on its way to capturing the Middle East hotel market.

Despite the boom in new hotels, elements of the past are often preserved, including local architecture and cultural traditions such as those seen at the superb Madinat Jumeirah complex. The result is a fascinating mix of the exotic sights and sounds of the souk and the timelessness of the desert and oases, combined with the comfort of luxurious hotels and restaurants of an international standard. There's also the added bonus of low-cost shopping for all kinds of products, be they gold, designer clothes, electronic goods, perfumes or handcrafted artefacts.

Madinat Jumeirah is one of Dubai's top tourist attractions and consists of two hotels, a souk, a theatre, an amphitheatre, a health club and more than 40 restaurants.

For many years the expatriate workforce, their families, visiting business people and diplomats enjoyed having the emirate as a virtually exclusive playground.

Vast swimming pools, health centres, spas and squash and tennis courts are nearly all standard at Dubai's five-star hotels, while those with their own beaches – such as the Jumeirah Beach Hotel – have numerous aquatic activities.

Discriminating travellers then began to discover that Dubai offered an alternative destination that was unspoilt, yet provided an abundance of leisure pursuits. Transit customers passing through Dubai International Airport were also alerted, by the bargains on offer in the duty-free shops, to the fact that Dubai was no ordinary shopping destination.

Building on the highly positive response of those first intrepid tourists, the local hotel and travel trade – particularly the Government of Dubai Department of Tourism and Commerce Marketing, Emirates airline and Dubai Duty Free – have conducted far-reaching marketing campaigns. Their success has made the emirate well known to both the international travel trade and individual travellers. Many international showbiz and sporting personalities who've visited Dubai have lavished praise on the emirate and this too has contributed to the positive international image.

It's easy to understand the appeal of Dubai, with visitors from Northern Europe particularly relishing the escape from freezing winter when the weather in the UAE is at its absolute best (from the beginning of November until March). During this period temperatures remain at about 26°C (80°F) and the humidity stays low.

Much of Dubai's diurnal social life still revolves round the five-star hotels and clubs that are among the best in the world. Swimming pools, health-and-fitness centres, spas and squash and tennis courts are nearly all standard hotel fixtures, while those with private beaches have sailing, parasailing, windsurfing, water-skiing and jet-skiing. But there are also a number of pleasant, uncrowded public beaches to choose from.

A busy sporting calendar

Dubai has an extensive and eventful sporting calendar, with numerous local and international events held throughout the year. Each new season starts with the onset of the cooler weather in October, when traditional dhow racing (both sailing and rowing forms), camel racing and horse racing commence in earnest.

The UAE Desert Challenge traditionally takes place in November, followed by the Dubai International Rally. Dubai then plays host to the IRB 7s World Series early in December, with the immensely popular Dubai Rugby 7s tournament, followed by the Dubai rounds of the UIM Class 1 Powerboat Championships.

The Dubai Marathon, held early in January each year, is the first of the international events of the new year, while two of Dubai's foremost sporting events, the Dubai Desert Classic and the Dubai Tennis Open are usually held between February and March. The climax of the sporting season – as well as the social season – is the Dubai World Cup, the world's richest horse race, held in March each year, which also marks the end of Dubai's horse-racing season.

On the greens

Dubai has pioneered the trend of creating golf courses in the deserts of Arabia, overcoming nature's objections with millions of litres of desalinated water. By 2007 there were five well-appointed clubs with six world-class, 18-hole championship grass courses situated within the emirate – enough to enjoy a different course each day of the week.

The regional golf revolution started in 1988 with the inauguration of the Emirates Golf Club, followed by the Dubai Creek Golf and Yacht Club five years later. For obvious reasons, the biggest challenge was planting grass that would stand a chance under the harsh summer sun. Yet not only has the carefully selected hybrid grass survived, it actually thrives when temperatures are at their highest and the greens have to be cut twice a day in the peak of summer.

'The Desert Miracle' was the name given to the landmark **Emirates Golf Club** when it became the first all-grass championship golf course in the Gulf. Its iconic clubhouse resembles a group of Bedouin tents, carved in white and standing out majestically against the emerald-green carpet laid before it. The club sports two championship courses.

In addition to its fine championship golf course and a nine-hole par-three course, the popular Dubai Creek Golf and Yacht Club boasts a superb marina, several restaurants, a hotel and 92 Arabian-style residential villas.

The Dubai Creek Golf &
Yacht Club is situated in
the heart of Dubai and is
easily recognized by its
iconic clubhouse which
takes the form of the
billowing sails of a dhow.

The original course – and home to the Dubai Desert Classic – is the Majlis
Course. Most of the world's top players have taken part in the Desert Classic and
it has become one of the European PGA Tour's top events. The club's second
championship course, the Wadi Course, was completed in 1996 before being
redesigned by Nick Faldo and re-opened in 2006.

Running along the stretch of water from which it takes its name, the **Dubai
Creek Golf & Yacht Club** was voted one of the top-100 'must-play' golf courses
in the world by the UK magazine *Golf World* and has twice hosted the Dubai
Desert Classic. This beautifully landscaped course was recently redesigned by
European Golf Design in association with locally based professional Thomas
Björn. The club features yet another iconic clubhouse, one that takes the form of
a dhow with sails full in the breeze. In addition to the course itself, there's also a
floodlit nine-hole, par-three course and driving range for playing or practising in
the cooler desert evenings, as well as the Park Hyatt Dubai hotel, 92 villas, a 121-
berth yacht marina and six restaurants.

Located in prestigious Emirates Hills and managed by Troon Golf, **The
Montgomerie, Dubai** combines Scottish links-style golf with boutique hotel
accommodation overlooking the championship course. Designed by Colin
Montgomerie, in association with Desmond Muirhead, the course features 81
bunkers and 14 lakes and adds a distinctive variety to the golfing landscape of
the region. One of the signature hole designs, the par-three 13th, is said to boast
the largest single green in the world.

The **Arabian Ranches Golf Club** was designed by Ian Baker-Finch in association with Nicklaus Design. Formerly known as The Desert Course, Arabian
Ranches, it was conceived as a true desert-style course similar to those found in
California and Arizona and has created an oasis effect through the Arabian
Ranches properties. Each of the club's golf carts has a GPS yardage system that
informs players of the exact distance from their cart to the centre of the green,
rather like a virtual caddy that constantly provides useful information. In addition
to all the usual facilities, the clubhouse has 11 luxurious, en-suite guest rooms.

At the time of going to press, Dubai's newest championship course was the Al

Badia Golf Resort, an 'oasis-themed' course designed by Robert Trent Jones II and located on the banks of Dubai Creek in the heart of Dubai Festival City. Villas with views of the golf, the lakes and the Dubai skyline are being built around the course.

A number of new golf courses are planned for Dubai. Already under development is The Dunes, located at Victory Heights within Dubai Sports City (itself a part of the massive Dubailand project). This championship course, scheduled to open towards the end of 2007, will carry the signature of three-times Dubai Desert Classic winner, Ernie Els, in association with Nicklaus Design.

However, this is by no means the only course being developed at Dubailand, where more than Dhs 6.5 billion has been earmarked towards creating Dubai Golf City, which will house no less than five themed signature courses, a golf academy, a resort hotel and spa, residential communities, golf villages and retail souks.

All of the above clubs boast an academy with full teaching facilities and friendly professionals cater for every level of golfer. The facilities are comparable to the best in the world. They also all have a choice of excellent dining facilities (some have several), as well as provision for many other sports and, as already mentioned, some even boast their own hotels or clubhouse accommodation.

Although the clubs operate on membership schemes, pay-and-play is available for those holding a current handicap card. This means that tourists, or even residents less dedicated to the game, can now play without making a substantial financial commitment. It's advisable, however – especially during the cooler winter months – to book in advance because of the game's extreme popularity. For the serious amateur player, competitions are organized throughout the region

Tiger Woods is a regular visitor to the Dubai Desert Classic, one of the European PGA Tour's top events, and he is also involved in one of Dubai's new golf courses.

Frankie Dettori, riding for the ruling family's Godolphin Stables, wins the 2006 Dubai World Cup on Electrocutionist. This was the third time Dettori won this race.

by the UAE Golf Association, which also plays a major role in the development of junior players.

To help meet the never-ending demand for facilities, the Jebel Ali Hotel has a nine-hole grass course in beautiful surroundings, with spectacular sea views from some of the greens.

Equestrian sports

Dubai's association with the world of horse racing is strong, thanks to the whole-hearted interest of the Maktoum family. The quest for excellence on the racetrack led to the foundation of the Godolphin Stables by the late Sheikh Maktoum bin Rashid Al Maktoum and his brother, Sheikh Mohammed bin Rashid Al Maktoum, himself a celebrated endurance rider.

When Sheikh Maktoum passed away in 2005, Sheikh Mohammed immediately changed the name of the Al Maktoum Challenge – the world's richest show-jumping event – to the Al Maktoum Memorial Challenge to honour his brother, a major contributor to the international and local thoroughbred horse-racing scene.

Nad Al Sheba racecourse, which opened in 1994, is just minutes from the city centre, offering superb facilities for horses, riders and spectators. Since 1996, it has been the venue for the world's richest horse race, the Dhs 22-million (US$6-million) Dubai World Cup. Run over a distance of 10 furlongs, the race is for four-year-olds and upwards. In its short history the Dubai World Cup has been a spectacular success, attracting crowds of up to 50,000 people. Normally, six other races are contested on World Cup Day, the total purse for all the races being a whopping Dhs 55 million (US$15 million)

Although gambling is not permitted, up to 15,000 spectators attend Dubai's weekly race meetings, which are held between October and March both at the Nad Al Sheba and the Jebel Ali track near Emirates Hills.

At the end of 2007 Dubai World Cup meeting, Sheikh Mohammed announced plans for the Meydan project – a major redevelopment of the entire Nad Al Sheba site to create a lavish horse-racing 'city'.

Endurance racing could be described as the equestrian equivalent of a marathon since most races are more than 120 kilometres in distance and require several hours to complete. The UAE is a world leader in the development of this form of racing thanks in no small part to the stamina of the Arabian horse that is so ideally suited to the desert terrain, and the passion of its riders, including members of the ruling families of the UAE. In fact, Sheikh Mohmammed bin Rashid Al Maktoum has a number of major endurance racing victories to his credit and his sons have topped the world rankings several time since 1999.

Water sports

Flanked by the warm, turquoise waters of the Gulf, Dubai provides the perfect opportunity for all forms of water sport, with clubs and societies galore.

One of the most challenging competitor sports is powerboat racing, with the Class One World Offshore Powerboat Championships among the major events on Dubai's sporting calendar. Thousands of fans gather to watch the world's top teams battle out the final rounds of the championship at the Dubai International Marine Club (DIMC) and the races bring a carnival atmosphere to the beach, with pop concerts between races.

Dubai's Victory Team is acknowledged as the most successful team in the history of offshore racing. With six class-one and four class-two world titles, the team has carried the UAE flag with determination. All the Victory boats are built and rigged entirely in their Dubai facility, adjacent to the DIMC.

Like all other forms of water sport, sailing is a favourite weekend activity in Dubai and DIMC, Dubai Offshore Sailing Club (DOSC) and Jebel Ali Sailing Club (JASC) all have marinas and organize numerous activities and competitions for enthusiasts. Plans for sailing developments in Dubai include the opening of a new state-of-the-art sailing academy and the expansion of the junior sailing programme that created the UAE national team.

DIMC was established in 1988 and is considered as the main driving force behind UAE water sport activities. It was the first Arab organization to be granted

In addition to horse racing, endurance racing and showjumping, polo is also popular in Dubai, with the Dubai Polo & Equestrian Club based at Arabian Ranches.

The shipwrecks off Dubai provide opportunities for scuba diving in warm, clear water. Several local dive schools provide international certification and arrange diving trips in the Arabian Gulf.

full membership of the Union Internationale Motonautique (UIM) and has staged a number of top-class international sailing events in recent years. These include the Dubai Junior Regatta, one of the world's top junior sailing festivals; the Maktoum Trophy, a rapidly emerging fleet-racing series; and the Dubai Match Race series. More international events can be expected in the future.

The decision by the America's Cup holder, *Alinghi*, to conduct an intensive winter training programme in Dubai prior to defending the cup in Valencia in 2007 was seen as a major endorsement of the facilities at DIMC, Dubai's sailing conditions and the emirate's plans to reinforce its position as a world-class venue for international sailing events.

Dubai boasts several fully equipped marinas where boats can be launched or hired for deep-sea fishing. The Gulf yields regular catches of sailfish, mackerel, barracuda, shark and many other varieties of fish.

Other aquatic activities include water-skiing, sail-boarding, jet-skiing, kite-boarding, para-sailing, scuba-diving (with much emphasis on the large number of shipwrecks close to Dubai), snorkelling and surfing. A number of these can be enjoyed on the beaches of Dubai's coastal hotels, where both equipment and tuition is available.

Racing on dunes and tarmac

Motor rallying flourishes in Dubai and the UAE. Launched in 1991, the UAE Desert Challenge, the final round of the FIA Cross Country Rally World Cup and the FIM Cross Country Rallies World Championship is held each November, attracting stars such as Stéphane Peterhansel, Dakar Rally winner in 2004 and 2005, who has won the Desert Challenge three times in recent years, and Jo Schlesser, who took the chequered flag five times between 1994 and 2001. Another international event is the UAE International Rally, while Dubai has the 1000 Dunes Rally, held in conjunction with the Dubai Shopping Festival, and the Dubai International Rally, won by Mohammed Ben Sulayem from 1985–8, 1991–5 and 1997–2002.

A household name in the UAE, Mohammed Ben Sulayem is a champion rally driver and a Dubai resident. He has won more FIA regional championships, and more international rallies, than any other rally driver in history. His premier contest has always been the FIA Middle East Rally Championship. Since first winning the championship in 1986, he has gone on to win it 14 times, having never been defeated. He took a sabbatical from racing after his 2002 season and is currently president of the Automobile and Touring Club of the UAE.

The new Dubai Autodrome and Business Park within Dubailand is the first motor-sport facility in the UAE meeting FIA standards. Incorporating a world-class racing track, a pit-lane complex of international standard, state-of-the-art grandstands, hospitality suites for corporate customers and a karting circuit, the venue has already attracted a number of exciting international events.

The Dubai Autodrome, a part of Dubailand, was the first motor-sport facility in the UAE to meet FIA standards and has hosted a number of exciting international events since it opened.

Traditional sports

The sport of falconry has existed for centuries in the UAE where the falcons most commonly used are the Hurr (Little Saker) and the Shaheen (Peregrine Falcon). According to the UAE office of the global conservation organization, WWF, hunting with falcons is allowed in UAE in the triangle between Al Ain, Dubai and Abu Dhabi, and the sport can be practised by the public during three months in winter. The main prey is the endangered Houbara Bustard, which winters in the emirates after arriving from Kazakhstan, China and Afghanistan.

Captive breeding of the Houbara is being undertaken at the National Avian Research Centre (NARC) of the Environment Agency in Abu Dhabi. With a mission to reconcile the tradition of Arab falconry with sustainable use of natural resources throughout the bustard's and falcon's range, the NARC started breeding attempts in 1993. Numbers have gradually increased and the aim is to raise 600–700 bustards annually. Re-introduction and re-stocking depleted Houbara populations for hunting or falcon training are among the objectives of this conservation initiative.

The camel is greatly admired and respected in the Gulf and camel racing, which has developed into a professional sport with significant prize money, preserves this heritage in the UAE and elsewhere. Nad Al Sheba is the home of camel racing in Dubai and has a large and well-equipped track which attracts UAE nationals, expatriate residents and adventurous tourists during the winter racing season. Racing camels are bred specifically for the sport and the best can change hands for staggering amounts.

Back in the 1980s, Dubai's deputy ruler, Sheikh Hamdan bin Rashid Al Maktoum, introduced dhow racing to revive both the emirate's historic link to the sea and the skills of local sailors. The first races, held in 1986, involved a few dhows that had survived from the days of sail. Since then, owners have been encouraged to build new boats without affecting the basic design used by their forefathers and DIMC inspects each racing dhow to ensure specifications are met, resulting in competition that is safe and fair, and calls on the skills of sailors of the past.

The dhow's hull must be constructed from teak, which may be varnished but not painted, the mast and bowsprit must also be wooden and the sails canvas. Lacking a weighted keel, large dhows are unstable. Traditionally, dhows stowed their heavy cargo low in the hold to assist with balance and today's racers use sandbags to perform the same task. As the wind freshens, these sandbags have to be shifted and crew members have to be positioned to keep the boat trimmed. If the wind dies, the captain can dump some sandbags overboard to increase speed, but if the wind freshens again the boat will be at risk of capsizing.

Dubai now has a substantial fleet of 60-foot, lateen-rigged dhows that race with a 12-man crew. There are two other classes; the 43-foot dhows race with a crew of 10, while the 22-foot dhows are manned by junior crews. At stake are pride and prestige; prize-money is the last consideration.

Horses, and especially the purebred Arabian, have played an important role in the history of the Arab World, most notably in hunting and combat, where their speed, agility and stamina were often the decisive factor between victory and defeat. It's not surprising, therefore, that the Arabian is another sporting link with the past. Stables in Dubai and elsewhere in the UAE – including many belonging to the ruling families – having been at the forefront of reintroducing the Arabian horse to Arabia are now passionately involved in improving the breed.

With its legendary stamina, the breed is ideally suited to endurance racing and is also making a mark in flat racing. Most race meetings in Dubai, including the World Cup, have a race reserved for Arabians.

Traditional sports such as falconry and camel racing – the former photographed at the Jumeirah Bab Al Shams Desert Resort & Spa – thrive in Dubai.

The annual Dubai Rugby 7s has been played since 1969 and is the opening round of the IRB World 7s Series as well as a great social weekend.

A pot-pourri of sport

Leaving traditional sports, football is probably the most popular sport among expatriate and national Arabs. The UAE FA was established in 1971 and Dubai boasts four magnificent football stadiums, home grounds of four clubs.

Two Dubai companies, Dubai Holding and Emirates airline, are major sponsors of football with the former sponsoring the UAE team. However, it was Emirates that signed the biggest sponsorship deal in history, worth Dhs 662 million (US$180 million) with the English premiership team, Arsenal. As part of the sponsorship agreement, Arsenal will set up a soccer school in the UAE, this being in addition to the Manchester United soccer school that will be based at Dubai Sports City in Dubailand.

Rugby has been played in Dubai since 1966. It is now enjoyed by men, women and juniors, the majority of them expatriates from Australia, New Zealand, South Africa and the UK, although more and more nationals are coming through at the junior level. Each winter Dubai competes against other emirates, Gulf cities and Gulf states, in the hope of winning the Arabian Gulf League and the Arabian Gulf Cup, while the Arabian Gulf also has a team that competes in international tournaments such as the IRB World 7s Series.

The Emirates Airline Dubai Rugby 7s, an annual tournament that has been played since 1969 – and the opening round of the IRB 7s World Series – has become one of the premier events of its kind. Sixteen of the best rugby-playing nations in the world fight it out for top honours in a competition that also sees Gulf, social, ladies, veterans, youth and international invitation teams on four grass fields.

More than 160 teams and 1,750 players strapped on their boots for the three-day rugby extravaganza in 2006, won by South Africa. No wonder it is one of the

Middle East's most popular social weekends of the year, attracting enthusiastic crowds of up to 30,000 spectators and being voted the 'Best Sporting Event' by the Dubai public in the What's On Awards from 2002–2007 inclusive.

Tennis, with the advantage that it can be played at night on floodlit courts, enjoys a longer season than most sports in Dubai. The Dubai Tennis Championships, owned and organized by Dubai Duty Free, were inaugurated in 1993. The 2007 championships saw the world number one, Roger Federer, win his fourth Dubai title in five years. Justine Henin-Hardenne won the women's final, beating Amelie Mauresmo, keeping her unbeaten record in the 16 matches she's played in Dubai and adding to the trophies she won in 2003, 2004 and 2006. Martina Hingis, Amelie Mauresmo and Lindsay Davenport have also won the women's championship in recent years.

Another world-class facility popular with tourists, business people and residents is the Jebel Ali Shooting Club. Traditional Arab forts were the inspiration behind the architecture, which houses what is arguably the most luxurious shooting club in the world. There's a strong emphasis on clay-pigeon shooting, catering for seven disciplines within the sport. Inside there's also a state-of-the-art, fully automated and air-conditioned pistol range. The simulator used by various police forces for training purposes is one of the club's main attractions.

Dubai's residents take full advantage of the emirate's magnificent parks and recreational grounds where informal football and cricket matches are a favourite pastime. Among the more surprising sports in Dubai are archery, ice-skating and snow skiing and boarding at the Ski Dubai facility in the Mall of the Emirates. In fact, it would seem that Dubai has something to suit everybody's taste.

Sport has always played a major role in the development of tourism in Dubai.

Most of the world's top male and female tennis players compete in the annual Dubai Tennis Championships, which were inaugurated in 1993.

The much-anticipated opening of the first integrated purpose-built sports venue in the world, Dubai Sports City, is scheduled for 2007. It will incorporate a Manchester United soccer school, a championship golf course designed by Ernie Els, a Butch Harmon golf academy, a David Lyons tennis stadium, and the offices of the International Cricket Council (ICC). Four stadiums with seating capacities from 8,000–25,000 will host World Cup-calibre rugby, football, cricket, hockey and athletics events. These, together with Dubai Golf City and other sporting attractions will play an important role in making Dubailand the world's leading destination for leisure and entertainment.

Indeed, with the growth of its sporting facilities, Dubai seems set to make a bid for the 2016 Olympics. However, the climate is simply too hot for the summer Olympics and the emirate would need to negotiate a spring or autumn date. Another potential disadvantage is that the UAE does not have a strong Olympic tradition, with only one summer Olympic Games medal in its history (won by Sheikh Ahmed bin Mohammed bin Hasher Al Maktoum for double trap shooting).

Exploring the interior

In addition to sport, Dubai is a marvellous place for leisure pursuits and virtually every type of leisure activity awaits the visitor.

The desert is the first thing most visitors want to see and for those who venture into the interior the results can be an eye-opener. Companies specializing in desert safaris employ expert drivers who also double as knowledgeable desert guides. Possibly the most popular type of safari is an evening trip into the desert to watch the sunset and then enjoy a barbecue or a traditional Arabic meal under the stars; complete with camel rides and belly-dancers.

On the other hand, many residents own 4x4s and prefer to go off-roading with friends in dune fields or in the mountains. Wadis (dried-up water courses) provide routes through these areas, just as they did in the past. It's a favourite way to escape at the weekend and can lead to the discovery of flora and fauna, places of historical interest such as old forts and watchtowers, and even refreshing natural, crystal-clear pools and waterfalls.

Favourite tourist spots

A favourite tourist destination for visitors to Dubai is the garden city of Al Ain, an hour's drive south-east of Dubai. Set among the lush greenery of several oases in the centre of the country, Al Ain is a rapidly developing tourist centre. It has a large zoo and wildlife park, a family amusement park, a fascinating museum and Hili Gardens – a beautifully landscaped area with an archaeological site of uncovered Bronze Age tombs and a reconstructed ancient village. However, most people are content to explore Al Ain's oases and old forts or to take a drive to the top of nearby Jebel Hafit.

Another popular area is the East Coast – a short drive across the peninsula. Fine beaches provide excellent swimming and snorkelling against the magnificent back-drop of the Hajar Mountains. Fishing and scuba diving can also be enjoyed off-shore, while there are a number of forts and watchtowers to be explored en route.

A worthwhile tourist stop in Dubai itself is the city's historical Al Fahidi Fort, close to the Creek; the fort has had a varied life as a garrison, arms store and jail but is now the city's museum, taking the visitor through a remarkable series of galleries with lifelike dioramas that recreate the Dubai of yesteryear.

Great efforts are being made to conserve Dubai's architectural heritage. Close to the Dubai Museum is an area of former merchants' wind-towered houses known as Bastikiya. These houses are currently being restored to their original state.

The Creekside Sheikh Saeed House, home of the Dubai ruling family until

Many Dubai residents own 4x4s and head for the mountains or dune fields during weekends (bottom). Visitors can also enjoy organized 4x4 outings, which often end in an evening of fun under the stars (top).

Dubai Museum is situated in the historic Al Fahidi Fort – the oldest building in Dubai.

1958, is another example of careful renovation. Built of coral blocks and decorated with intricate cornices and plaster screens, it forms a beautiful addition to the Creek's waterfront in the Shindagha district.

The adjacent Dubai Heritage Village is worth a visit, especially during the Dubai Shopping Festival and other celebrations when it hosts numerous cultural events. The Village provides an insight into Dubai's traditional culture and lifestyle, with folk dancing, music and Emirati cuisine some of the main attractions.

Dubai Creek itself can be enjoyed from an *abra* (water taxi) or on a sunset or dinner cruise aboard a motorized dhow. Other craft whisk passengers through the mouth of the Creek into the Arabian Gulf.

International entertainers

In complete contrast to the tranquillity and solitude of the desert, Dubai offers an extensive concert programme, ranging from the classical to nostalgic and modern. Over the years, top pop stars such as Elton John, Mark Knopfler, Shakira, Sting and Robbie Williams have visited the emirate and staged first-class shows that have helped Dubai become the Gulf's leading entertainment centre.

Striving to be the best live act in Dubai, an impressive line-up of resident bands perform nightly in restaurants and popular nightspots, ensuring a high standard and great choice in live music throughout the week. In addition to opera and ballet, residents and visitors have been able to choose from string quartets, chamber orchestras and classical soloists such as Julian Lloyd Webber and Vanessa Mae. Each of The Three Tenors – Jose Carreras, Placido Domingo and Luciano Pavarotti – has performed as an individual in Dubai, as have all of Arabia's top artistes.

The Madinat Theatre at Madinat Jumeirah presents an enticing selection of quality productions, including comedy, drama and musicals while, on the Asian

front, film stars, musicians, dancers and ghazal singers all visit Dubai, frequently attracting mammoth audiences.

As if all this imported talent was not enough, the local and expatriate communities have formed a plethora of clubs that allow residents to follow their own particular interests. These range from art circles, language associations, history societies, amateur dramatics and singing clubs, to a flying school, motoring and equestrian clubs and natural-history groups. And, of course, there are many social, beach and sports associations at private or hotel clubs to choose from.

The Gulf Art Fair, launched in 2007, provided an opportunity for more than 40 of the world's leading art dealers to display and sell a variety of work.

81

The hotels of Dubai

If, as the maxim goes, the three main features of a property are 'location, location, location', Dubai is perfectly situated to offer an interesting range of holidays. From beach resorts to city hotels – and even a desert resort or two – visitors are spoilt for choice. Throw in a few specialities, such as a world-class spa here, a golf resort there – and you'll see why so many leading international hotel chains are already represented in Dubai . . . and why those that aren't soon will be.

As in any emerging market, Dubai's hotel developments have mostly been within the five-star range and, although many more spectacular luxury hotels are being constructed, the future is also likely to see an increase in the number of mid-range branded hotels. Another new trend is for 'designer' hotels such as the first Armani hotel (to be housed in the world's tallest building, the Burj Dubai) and the Palazzo Versace Dubai which promises a temperature-controlled beach.

Many of Dubai's new hotels will be situated in mega developments such as The Palm, The World, Dubailand and Burj Dubai. The Palm Jumeirah, for example, is creating a destination of world-class hotels including the Chedi, Dusit, Fairmont, Hilton, Jumeirah, Marriott, Metropolitan, Mövenpick, Oberoi, One&Only, Radisson SAS, Shangri-La and Starwood brands – nearly all of which already have properties elsewhere in Dubai. Two landmark properties on the Crescent of the island will be the Taj Exotica Resort & Spa and Atlantis The Palm. The Palm Trump International Hotel and Tower will be the anchor building of the Palm Golden Mile, located on the trunk of the Palm Jumeirah.

For those who would like to try a local hotel group, the Abu Dhabi-based Rotana Hotels has several excellent properties in Dubai while the local Dutco Hotels has the Jebel Ali Golf Resort and Spa, Hatta Fort Hotel (Dubai's only mountain resort hotel) and the Oasis Beach Hotel. However, it is Dubai's own Jumeirah hotel group that is leading the way. . . .

Icons of a modern city

The Jumeirah hotel group, formerly known as Jumeirah International, was established in 1997 with the opening of the Jumeirah Beach Hotel and today boasts some of the best hotels in the world.

A feature of the Jumeirah properties is their stunning architecture, making them icons of Dubai. Jumeirah Beach Hotel is designed in the shape of a breaking wave; Burj Al Arab, built on a man-made island, is designed in the shape of a billowing sail and reflects the region's maritime heritage; while Jumeirah Emirates Towers, a striking complex in the heart of Dubai's commercial district, consists of the Jumeirah Emirates Towers Hotel and Emirates Towers Offices – until recently the tallest building in the Middle East and Europe.

Jumeirah's other Dubai properties include the Jumeirah Beach Club Resort & Spa, Jumeirah Bab Al Shams Desert Resort & Spa and Madinat Jumeirah, an Arabian resort that, happily for those not staying at the resort, can be enjoyed by everyone. It consists of two 'grand boutique hotels' (Mina A'Salam and Al Qasr), a souk styled on traditional lines, the Madinat Theatre, an amphitheatre, a health-club, more than 40 restaurants catering for all tastes, and conference and banqueting facilities. Hotel guests can enjoy a kilometre of private beach and the complex adjoins Burj Al Arab and Jumeirah Beach Hotel as well as Jumeirah's Wild Wadi Water Park.

In 2001 Jumeirah expanded into Europe, taking over management of the Carlton Tower and the Lowndes Hotel in London. It has since added Jumeirah Essex House in New York to its portfolio and the HanTang Jumeirah Shanghai is expected to open in China in 2008. Another London hotel, the Jumeirah Hotel at Beetham Towers is planned and further rapid growth is most likely.

Chapter Eight
Shopping

Shoppers are spoilt for choice in Dubai. Looking for gifts or good buys becomes particularly enjoyable because shopping in the emirate is a varied and fascinating experience, ranging from bargain-priced electrical goods to exquisite Persian rugs. In fact, many travellers say that shopping is one of their main reasons for coming to Dubai. Traditional souks, modern shopping malls and Dubai Duty Free have earned Dubai the title 'shopper's paradise'.

Some 70 new malls and expansion projects are scheduled to be completed in the GCC by 2008 and Retail International, a British shopping mall consultancy, has estimated that Dubai will have the highest retail spend in the GCC by 2009 – even higher than in Saudi Arabia which has a greater population – because of the retail income generated by tourists.

Dubai's long summer is one of the main reasons for its vibrant 'mall culture'. This is a time when most people choose to stay indoors and the shopping malls provide an attractive environment to do just this, being 'cool' in both senses of the word, with easy access and parking, numerous lifts and escalators, a pleasant ambience and a vibrant cafe-society atmosphere.

Mall of the Emirates, one of the largest shopping centres in the world outside North America, has more than 400 shops in addition to a cinema complex, restaurants, a theatre, a five-star hotel and the Middle East's first indoor ski resort.

Some 200 outlets are found in Dubai's Gold Souk, each stocking up to 50 kilograms of gold jewellery, giving Dubai the name 'City of Gold'.

Endless choice

So where do you start? The choice is endless and includes gold, precious stones, exquisite silks and brocades, seductive perfumes and the latest designer wear from the world's top fashion houses. An astonishing array of cameras, pens, computers, furniture and traditional souvenirs are also available. Artefacts from round the world can be purchased from galleries throughout the metropolis.

Various stores stock leather goods, fine crystal and porcelain, elaborately embossed and marvellously wrought. Shoppers can wander through bright, stylish interiors decorated with lush plants and cool fountains or meander through bustling souks in narrow streets; each shop has its own character, enticing people to spend.

A watch for every occasion can be bought and it's been said that there are more shops selling watches in Dubai than there are supermarkets (but then you can also buy watches at supermarkets). Ticking away at various outlets are classic and exclusive collections from the world's finest manufacturers.

Warm, lingering, sensuous perfumes filled with the heady fragrance of spices are a hallmark of the Middle East, with frankincense a traditional example. In Dubai the variety of perfumes, some presented in flasks of sterling silver or gold, is endless while all the very latest Western brands are available.

History and tradition

Carpets call for special skills in weaving, design and colouring and you can find

valuable collector's items as well as functional rugs in brilliant designs and colours. Shyam Ahuja rugs in pastel shades, Iranian and Kashmiri carpets in traditional Persian designs, as well as kilims handcrafted in cotton, wool or silk are all available, in addition to handmade carpets from China and machine-made examples from Egypt, Romania, Hungary and other European countries.

For the enthusiastic souvenir hunter, Dubai has an endless variety of merchandise. The avid antique collector can find magnificent Omani bridal chests made of wood and decorated with ornate brass, traditionally used for storing clothes and jewellery, as well as Arabian coffee pots (*dallas*) in a variety of simple styles or adorned with silver and gold chains. There are also saddlebags, leather aprons, incense burners and camel decorations woven from goats' hair and dyed in brilliant colours.

Another traditional buy is the *khanjar*, a short curved dagger in an elaborately wrought sheath. Ancient rifles, muzzle-loading guns, falconry accoutrements, silver boxes and pearling knives used by divers are some of the treasures to be found in the souks.

Traditional Bedouin jewellery made of silver and encrusted with semi-precious stones is also a good buy, while bracelets, necklaces, brooches, belts, toe-rings and kohl containers all make ideal gifts.

None of Dubai's souks are more evocative than the Textile Souk, where there's a lot more to see than just textiles when exploring its alleys.

All that glitters . . .

Dubai is truly a city of gold. It's the third-largest centre in the world for gold bullion, after London and Zurich. Concentrated in the Gold Souk, an area that can be crossed in just 10 minutes, are 200 outlets, each stocking up to 50 kilograms of gold jewellery, giving Dubai the name 'City of Gold'. Also worth visiting are the retail outlets and manufacturers at the Gold & Diamond Park, adjacent to Sheikh Zayed Road and close to a number of hotels and Mall of the Emirates.

Gold also dazzles the visitor in the souks of Deira, where shop windows display chains, bangles, pendants, rings and necklaces. Dubai offers the widest range of gold jewellery in 18-, 21-, 22- and 24-carat gold, in styles that appeal to all nationalities, from the major jewellery centres of the world. As if all this is not enough, the new gold souk planned for Dubai Mall promises to be the largest in the world.

Setting the style

Many of Dubai's shopping malls have been built during the past few years, designed with the shopper's convenience as the primary consideration. No expense has been spared to make these new additions to the city's shopping scene luxurious and stylish, while ensuring a number maintain the hospitable ambience of the more traditional souks.

Situated in the heart of Bur Dubai and claiming to be 'the world's most luxurious shopping destination', BurJuman has more than 300 prestigious stores including Saks 5th Avenue. Flooded with sunlight, the centre's atrium courtyards have comfortable seating and abundant foliage, creating a relaxed yet vibrant shopping environment.

BurJuman will appeal to the fashion aficionado with Etienne Aigner, Bally, Hugo Boss, Bugatti, Burberry, Cartier, Just Cavalli, Chanel, Christian Dior, DKNY, Dolce & Gabbana, Alfred Dunhill, Escada, Etro, Salvatore Ferragamo, Hermes, Donna Karan, Calvin Klein, Christian Lacroix, Loewe, MaxMara, Mont Blanc, Prada, Polo Ralph Lauren, Tiffany & Co, Emanel Ungaro, Valentino, Van Cleef &

A relaxed environment is a feature of BurJuman's atrium courtyard. All of Dubai's shopping malls are popular destinations for summer outings.

Arpels, Versace, Louis Vuitton and Stuart Weitzman just some of the brands represented, as well as popular ready-to-wear apparel from the likes of Liz Claiborne, Kenneth Cole, Diesel, Elle, Esprit, Gap, Guess, Lacoste and Next.

Despite all the new competition, Deira City Centre is probably Dubai's busiest shopping mall and is home to more than 340 outlets. Its anchor stores include the French hypermarket Carrefour and the UK's Debenhams, situated on three floors. From high-end brands such as Burberry and Calvin Klein, to street fashion such as Gap, Mango and Zara, and with Arabian, jewellery and textile courts, City Centre's attraction lies in its sheer variety of stores and goods. The centre also has the Sofitel City Centre hotel, an 11-screen CineStar cinema complex, restaurants and a vast fast-food court. It's also an exciting place for children, who'll enjoy Dubai's largest indoor-entertainment and leisure complex.

The layout of one of the newest shopping malls in Dubai, Ibn Battuta Mall, is inspired by the legendary Arab explorer of the same name, with shopping courts themed around his world travels. The six attractive courts within the mall include architectural elements reminiscent of the Andalusian, North African, Egyptian, Persian, Indian and Chinese regions. Within Ibn Battuta's walls is the UAE's largest cinema, a 21-screen Megaplex with a Grand IMAX theatre.

The Mall of the Emirates, one of the largest shopping malls in the world outside of America, boasts more than 400 shops, a 14-screen cinema complex, a theatre, restaurants and a five-star Kempinski hotel. However, it is Ski Dubai, the first indoor ski resort in the Middle East (perhaps the third largest in the world, with five different ski-runs and a snow play area) that differentiates the mall from other newly completed malls in Dubai and the surrounding emirates.

The shopping mix – one of the best in Dubai – includes numerous high-end stores, the upmarket retailer, Harvey Nichols, Debenhams, Carrefour and the largest Virgin Megastore in the Middle East. Opened late in 2005, Mall of the Emirates enjoyed more than 10-million visitors in its first six months and expects

Ibn Battuta Mall, inspired by the travels of the legendary Arab explorer of the same name, is the largest single-floor mall in the world.

to attract 30-million visitors a year.

The atmospheric Souk Madinat Jumeirah is part of the Madinat Jumeirah Beach Resort, a recreation of classic Arabia with a modern twist. Situated next to the Burj Al Arab, along the beachfront, this upscale souk has all the flavour of a traditional bazaar with 75 open-fronted shops and galleries spilling onto air-conditioned walkways. Shoppers will delight in the unique handcrafted fare and numerous cafes, bars and restaurants along the one-kilometre-long shopping promenade.

Wafi City, topped by glass pyramids, hosts more than 200 upmarket stores that sell, among other products, fine leather garments, traditional carpets, French lingerie, children's toys and high-tech executive gifts. It also has a Marks & Spencer store and the best delicatessen in town. The beautiful sky-lit atrium creates a cool, spacious ambience and the centre also incorporates restaurants, cafes, a spa, leisure club and family entertainment centre.

Another exciting retail, dining and leisure attraction is the shopping district at Dubai Festival City. The colourful Festival Waterfront Centre brings together a selection of 550 shops, 90 restaurants, cafes and bistros, a 12-screen cinema complex and entertainment centre; while the Festival Power Centre is the largest household shopping centre in the UAE. The first HyperPanda hypermarket in the UAE, a flagship Plug-Ins showroom, the largest Ace Hardware and Garden Centre outside North America and the country's largest Ikea furniture store are open for business in the Festival Power Centre where 50 convenience and lifestyle stores complete the offering.

Shopping Districts

Just like all major centres, Dubai has some distinct shopping districts, far away from the bustle of the malls. Karama and Satwa are paradises for bargain finders, with every conceivable household accessory and knick knack available at very reasonable prices.

Two districts in Bur Dubai (Bank Street and the Golden Sands area) have 'computer souks' where you can buy every conceivable item of computer hardware and software. A visit to the 'Electronics Souk' in Al Fahidi Street near the Creek in Bur Dubai reveals a host of small shops selling everything from mini-calculators to the latest digital cameras.

Deira is often deemed 'the old part of town' and quite rightly so, considering its history and heritage. Here the Gold and Spice souks take you back to the days of old Arabia as you view row upon row of gold rings, bracelets, necklaces and ornaments; and enjoy the heady aromas of coriander, cinnamon, nutmeg, frankincense and myrrh.

Into the future

Most of Dubai's newer shopping malls have distinct themes. Ibn Battuta is the largest themed mall in the Middle East; Mall of the Emirates is planned around themed precincts reflecting the heritage of the region and forming streets, plazas and town squares; Souk Madinat Jumeirah exudes traditional Arab market charm and Wafi City reflects an Egyptian concept. Another fine example is Mercato Mall, with its distinctive Renaissance architecture, that makes it stand out from all the other smaller malls along Jumeirah Road, and has Italian, French and Spanish characteristics. Many of Dubai's future malls are likely to follow similar themes.

Nevertheless, the two most eagerly awaited malls in Dubai are not competing in terms of themes but for the title of 'the largest shopping mall in the world'. These are the Mall of Arabia and Dubai Mall.

The Mall of Arabia is an important part of the US$5-billion Dubailand complex. It will cover an area of nearly a million square metres, have four levels, more than

Two of Dubai's most popular shopping malls are the Egyptian-themed Wafi City, with its vibrant stained-glass windows (top), and the Festival Waterfront Centre at Dubai Festival City, which opened in 2007.

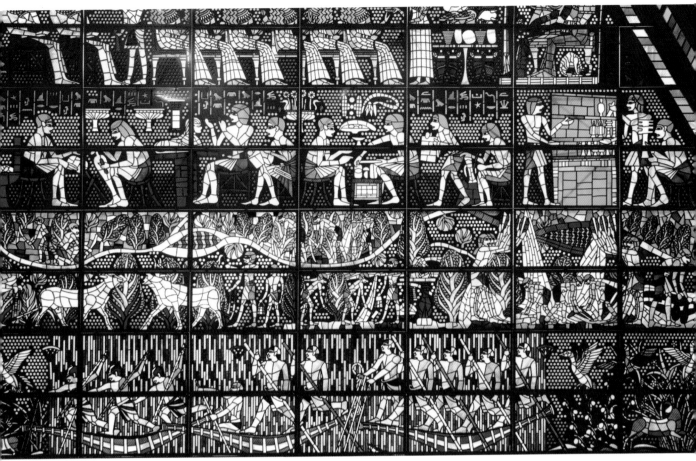

Launched in 1996 the annual Dubai Shopping Festival, which takes place from mid-January to mid-February, attracts thousands of visitors.

1,000 retail outlets and a 15-screen cinema complex. The retail outlets will be grouped together according to type and will include the top brands in luxury goods, household items, consumer electronics, children's toys and more. The mall's themed zones will also contain restaurants, cafes, and entertainment areas. The shopping mall will be circular in shape with an ancient Middle Eastern exterior, two rooftop hotels, and a vast theatre and auditorium at its centre. The mall will also be the point of entry and departure for the Restless Planet dinosaur park, which is being designed in collaboration with the Natural History Museum of London.

The Dubai Mall, despite its grand scale, is only one element of Emaar's sprawling Downtown Dubai district that will also feature Burj Dubai, the world's tallest tower. The mall will be the size of 50 'international-sized soccer pitches' and more than 1,000 stores, in 10–15 'malls-within-a mall', will form the centrepiece of the mall. Featured attractions, in addition to the world's largest gold souk already mentioned, will be one of the world's largest aquariums, an Olympic-sized ice-skating rink, a waterfall and a view of Burj Dubai.

Shopping festivals

Since its inception in 1996, the Dubai Shopping Festival has embodied the entre-preneurial spirit of Dubai. The result of the combined efforts of the government and the private sector, the festival occupies a full month in Dubai's busy calendar of annual events and takes place from mid-January to mid-February.

The festival draws attention from all over the world, both for the hundreds of special promotions offered on a vast array of goods and for its visual entertain-ment, ranging from magnificent fireworks displays over the Creek, and captivating laser shows, to bungee jumping, colourful street parades and the multicultural

Global Village.

Dubai Summer Surprises is the summertime counterpart of the Dubai Shopping Festival, with special events in the malls and themes changing weekly. It also has a strong family emphasis, focusing on both fun and education, and is especially popular with visitors from other parts of the Gulf.

Duty-free bonanza

From its launch in 1983, Dubai Duty Free has matured into a company with an annual turnover of nearly US$712 million. This turnover was achieved in 2006 and represented a 20-per-cent increase on the previous year.

Dubai Duty Free is widely recognized as one of the top airport-retail operations in the world and has been the recipient of numerous international awards. It provides travellers with a convenient shopping experience. Prices are kept low because the complex is operated directly by the Department of Civil Aviation, thereby cutting out concession fees. Many of the goods on offer are cheaper than in their country of origin and there is also a smaller, inbound duty free shop in the arrivals hall.

While Dubai Duty Free's record-breaking figures make interesting reading, the breakdown of certain sales categories for 2005 reveals some fascinating trivia. In that year the operation sold 3,781 kilograms of gold, 1,567,040 bottles of perfume, 2,263,487 cartons of cigarettes, 86,000 mobile phones and more than 160,000 watches.

Everything about Dubai International Airport is state-of-the-art, but behind the various facilities is a tradition of trading, of openness towards the rest of the world and, above all, of service – all of which, of course, have been the hallmarks of Dubai for centuries.

In terms of turnover, Dubai Duty Free is the third-largest outlet of its type in the world and has done much to attract tourists to the emirate.

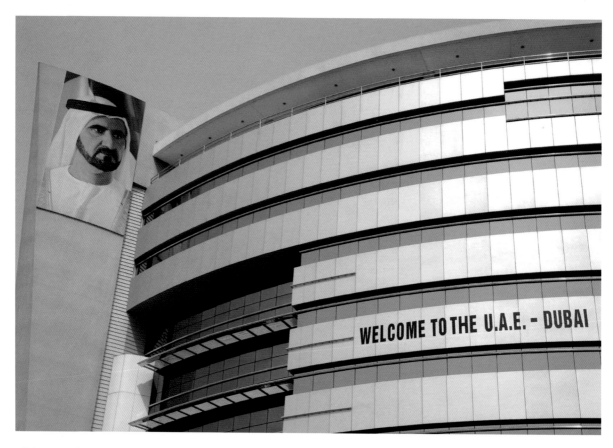

Chapter Nine
Tourist information

A sign near Dubai International Airport welcomes visitors to the city and provides them with a photo of its Ruler, Sheikh Mohammed bin Rashid Al Maktoum, who is also the Vice-President and Prime Minister of the UAE.

Dubai has developed into one of the world's major tourist destinations. With relaxed visa regulations, one of the most modern airports in the world, and almost all the airlines having direct flights, it's easily accessible. Whether you want to visit one of the many malls or souks, enjoy the sand dunes or the lush green parks, the city represents a seamless blend between the traditional and the contemporary. As the modern-day metropolis of the region, it bridges the east and the west while remaining rooted in its Islamic culture and heritage.

Banks and money exchanges

Most international banks have offices in Dubai or in the other emirates. Banking hours are from 08h00 to 14h00, Saturday through to Wednesday, with shorter hours on Thursday, closing at 13h00. However banks such as Citibank, which is open until 20h00, and Standard Chartered, until 15h30, operate longer. During Ramadan, the timings are from 09h00 to 13h00. Visitors should check locally. Most currencies can be freely converted in Dubai and you'll find reliable money-exchange outlets all over the city and its shopping malls.

Business hours

All government offices and most private-sector companies are closed on Fridays and Saturdays. Shops and supermarkets are open seven days a week, usually from 10h00 to 22h00, although some establishments start business on Fridays after noon prayers or even later in the evening.

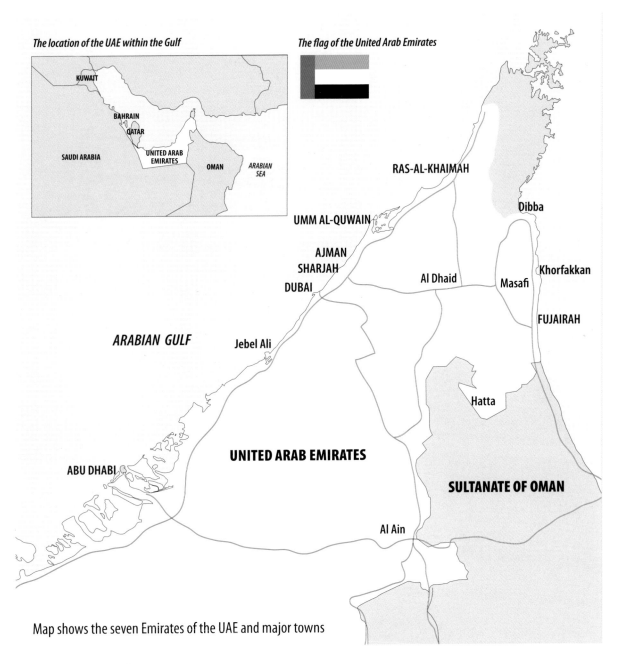

The location of the UAE within the Gulf

The flag of the United Arab Emirates

Map shows the seven Emirates of the UAE and major towns

Business services

Most hotels provide a range of business services for the business visitor to Dubai, while certain hotels are specially geared for business travellers. Temporary office space, meeting rooms, secretaries, translators, word and data processing, fax machines, Internet, e-mail and conference facilities are all available.

Climate

Dubai enjoys warm, sunny days and pleasantly cool evenings from October to April. The evenings in January and February can be chilly. From May onwards it's hot with temperatures reaching up to 120°F (47°C) or more in some desert areas during July and August. Humidity can also be very high from June to October, peaking in September. Shops, offices, banks, hotels and cars are air-conditioned, but most residents prefer to take their leave during the summer months to escape the heat. At this time Dubai becomes noticeably quieter.

	Daily max °C	Daily min °C	Sunshine (mean daily hours)	Rainfall (mean no of days with rain)
Jan	24	14	7.8	1.3
Feb	25	14	8.0	3.3
Mar	28	17	8.1	2.1
Apr	32	19	9.5	1.4
May	36	23	11.1	0.3
Jun	41	29	11.3	nil
July	41	29	10.3	nil
Aug	41	29	10.3	0.1
Sep	37	23	10.2	nil
Oct	37	23	9.8	nil
Nov	30	18	9.4	0.3
Dec	26	15	8.2	1.3

Clothing

Light clothing, preferably cotton and cotton mixes are suitable all year round, but sometimes it can get chilly during winter and a jacket may be required in the night. Beachwear is acceptable at swimming pools, on the beach and at hotels. But modesty in dress is recommended and appreciated at all times, especially in the rural areas.

Communications

Etisalat, the national telephone company, provides an excellent international direct-dialling system and international direct-dial telephones are available in the majority of hotel rooms. In addition, several hotels rent mobile telephones.

Landline calls within each emirate are free. Full telex, fax and e-mail facilities are widely available. Most local hotels provide guests with Internet facilities at nominal rates and there are many Internet cafes situated in the city. The mobile standard is GSM.

Since 2007, the UAE communications industry has been served by a second company, du, which delivers a complete range of telecommunications and entertainment services, from mobile to broadband Internet, TV, video and others.

Credit cards

Most retail establishments, hotels, restaurants and car-hire companies accept recognized international credit cards such as Visa, MasterCard, American Express and Diners Club, but some retailers offer better value for cash.

Currency

The official currency of the UAE is the dirham, which is divided into 100 fils and is fixed against the US dollar at approximately Dhs 3.67. There are no currency import or export restrictions. Notes are issued in denominations of five, 10, 20, 50, 100, 200 and 500 and 1,000 dirhams. One-dirham coins are also issued as well as smaller denominations.

The GCC plans to introduce a monetary union in 2010. Economists consider the devaluation of the dirham in such a context unlikely. Rather, the dirham is likely to be upwardly revalued alongside fellow Gulf currencies (such as the Saudi riyal) against the US dollar. At present the dirham is artificially undervalued and this contributes to high inflation and low interest rates. A unified GCC currency with its own central bank would set an interest rate and currency value more in line with local circumstances.

Customs

In addition to tobacco and perfumes, the Dubai Duty Free shop offers a varied choice of alcoholic drinks for departing and arriving non-Muslim passengers. Customs officials on entry may check videotapes, magazines and books and penalties for the illegal importation of drugs are severe.

Driving

For people of many nationalities, driving licences can be arranged locally on production of a valid passport and an international driving licence. Two passport photos are required. Roads and highways are generally excellent and signs are posted in Arabic and English. Speed limits are well marked and strictly enforced. Caution is required, especially at night, when driving through rural areas in which camels abound.

At the time of writing Dubai was suffering from severe traffic congestion as well as (by international standards) abnormally poor – and even dangerous – driving habits. Both problems were being addressed by the relevant authorities, with new roads and bridges being built, toll roads coming into effect and the Dubai Metro in advanced stages of construction.

Electricity

The domestic supply in Dubai and the United Arab Emirates is 220/240 volts at 50 cycles AC.

Residents and visitors make full use of Dubai's warm weather and seawater to enjoy time at the emirates fine beaches, including this one at Jebel Ali.

Cirque du Soleil's *Quidam* is just one of the top international acts to have visited Dubai. Here, an acrobat performs amazing stunts on the German wheel.

Entertainment

Dubai hosts world-renowned events, particularly from November through to March. Throughout the emirate, drama, poetry and folklore groups perform regularly. Top international entertainers, singers, musicians, dancers, actors and comedians also visit the emirate. In addition, there are concerts performed by classical musicians from all round the world, circuses, fashion fairs, trade exhibitions and various sporting events. There's also superb entertainment in a number of nightclubs, restaurants and discotheques. An experience not to be missed is a trip into the desert. Tour operators have full programmes of safaris undertaken in 4x4s by professional driver-guides.

Entry

There are several types of visas for visitors to Dubai and the situation changes as improvements are made and the process is streamlined. Airlines may require confirmation that the sponsor is holding a valid visa for the incoming visitor and a penalty charge of Dhs 100 a day is imposed on visitors who overstay.

Citizens of the GCC member states – Bahrain, Kuwait, Oman, Qatar and Saudi Arabia – do not need a visa, while GCC expatriate residents who meet certain conditions may obtain a non-renewable 30-day visa on arrival at the approved ports of entry.

Citizens of the UK (with the right of abode in the United Kingdom, as well as UK overseas passport holders born in China or Hong Kong), Andorra, Australia, Austria, Belgium, Brunei, Canada, Denmark, Finland, France, Germany, Greece, Holland, Iceland, Ireland, Italy, Japan, Liechtenstein, Luxembourg, Malaysia, Monaco, New Zealand, Norway, Portugal, San Marino, Singapore, South Korea, Spain, Sweden, Switzerland, USA and the Vatican City will be granted a free-of-

charge Visit Visa at any UAE port of entry. The visa enables them to stay for 60 days and may be renewed once for a period of 30 days for a fee of Dhs 500. Israeli nationals and holders of Hong Kong and UK Certification of Identification will not be issued visas.

Visitors from other countries requiring information on Entry-Service Permits, Visit Visas, Tourist Visas, Multiple-Entry Visas and Transit Visas should contact their travel agent, airline or an overseas office of the Government of Dubai Department of Tourism and Commerce Marketing. Please contact the Dubai Naturalization and Residency Administration Department or the nearest UAE Embassy for the latest information. Telephone: (+9714) 3980000, e-mail: ednrd@datelservice.com or visit the website at: www.dnrd.ae.

Food

In addition to local favourites such as *kabsa* (a whole sheep stuffed with rice, spices and almonds), *fattoush* salad and desserts such as *umm ali* (milk and sultana pudding) and *monbahalabia* (camel-milk cream with rose-water) virtually every kind of cuisine imaginable can be found in the emirate and there's a wide range of prices to suit every pocket. Visitors to Dubai should note that restaurants not attached to the airport, hotels and sports clubs are usually not licensed to serve alcohol.

Health

Although Dubai's hospitals are modern and well-equipped, private treatment is expensive, so many residents carry medical insurance and tourists are advised to take out their own medical insurance prior to travel. Pharmacies are comprehensively stocked and a number are open throughout the night.

Dubai offers diners an excellent choice of restaurants – with prices to suit all pockets – and a chance to sample the unique cuisine of the Middle East and the Gulf.

The beautiful Jumeirah Mosque has become a landmark on Dubai's Jumeirah Beach Road. Non-Muslims, too, can practise their faith freely in various places of worship in Dubai.

Language
Arabic is the national language but English, Hindi and Urdu are widely spoken. Most shopkeepers and hotel staff speak English. Telephone services employ English-speaking personnel.

Liquor
Alcohol is forbidden to Muslims but permitted for non-Muslims. There is a wide range of alcoholic beverages available in hotel restaurants and bars. Resident non-Muslims can apply for a licence for home consumption, but drinking alcohol in public is strictly forbidden.

Local time

The UAE is four hours ahead of GMT.

Newspapers and magazines

There are a number of Arabic-language newspapers: *Al Bayan, Al Ittihad, Al Khaleej, Al Fajer, Al Wahda* and *Emarat Al Youm,* as well as several national daily English-language newspapers: *Gulf News, Khaleej Times, The Gulf Today, Emirates Today* and *7Days.* Others come and go. English magazines published locally contain information on current events, commercial news and entertainment. *What's On* is a useful leisure and entertainment guide while *Gulf Business* deals with the Gulf region's main business developments and issues.

Photography

Photography is forbidden near government installations, but otherwise opportunities are endless and fascinating. From the souks and the desert to the Creek and dhows there's an amazing range of subjects. Always ask before taking photographs of any person and avoid taking photos of women.

Radio

UAE Radio in Dubai broadcasts news, music and interviews both in English and Arabic. English-language stations include Dubai FM, broadcasting on 92.0 FM, Channel 4 on 104.8 FM and the two Emirates stations, Radio 1 and 2, broadcasting on 104 and 99.3 FM respectively, along with talk radio, Dubai Eye, on 103.8.

Ramadan

Ramadan is the holy month of fasting, when Muslims abstain from eating, drinking or smoking till sunset. Non-Muslims are required to respect Ramadan practices by not eating, drinking, or smoking in front of Muslims or in public view during daytime. Appropriate dress is also appreciated. Restaurants and coffee shops remain closed till the evening iftar, when the fast is broken, and many stay open into the early morning hours. Although hotels serve food in a location screened from public view during this time, they do not serve alcohol. Working hours are reduced in most places. During this period, no live performances are held and loud music is not allowed.

Religion

Islam is the official religion of the country. The deep faith of Muslims is embodied in omnipresent mosques, serene and beautiful with minarets exquisitely designed and surmounted by cupolas and crescents. The muezzin calls the faithful to prayer five times a day. The holy day of rest is Friday. Non-Muslims can practise their faith in various places of worship.

Security

Dubai is an unusually safe and friendly city where tourists and residents can safely walk about late at night.

Shopping

As covered in chapter eight of this book, the choice for the shopper in Dubai is unlimited. The Dubai Shopping Festival, held during winter, has developed into a comprehensive tourism project, with attractive discounts, promotions and raffle draws to lure shoppers. Coupled with Dubai Summer Surprises, which keeps shoppers busy in summer, the city truly lives up to its image of a shopping destination.

Sports

Football, golf, hockey, tennis, squash, cricket, badminton, motor sports, go-karting, scrambling and cycling are all well represented in the UAE. There are numerous well-equipped clubs catering for the visitor who can take advantage of both indoor and outdoor activities. Top hotels have private beaches where the water-sport enthusiasts can kitesurf or windsurf, snorkel, sail, jet-ski and water-ski. Fishing and diving trips and charters can also be arranged. Keen sports enthusiasts can avail themselves of tennis courts and gymnasiums, where most hotels employ private instructors. Those preferring a more relaxing holiday can enjoy the swimming pool available at just about every upscale hotel.

In winter camel races are held throughout the UAE, during the weekends, and are always well attended. Horse races, including the spectacular Dubai World Cup, take place in winter between October and March.

There are two ice rinks, one at Al Nasr Leisureland and the other at Hyatt Regency Hotel. Both rinks give lessons for beginners. Skiers can practise their skills on the slopes throughout the year at Dubai's newest leisure and sport addition, Ski Dubai, 10-pin bowling can be enjoyed at Thunderbowl, and water lovers can enjoy, splashing around Wild Wadi Water Park.

Television

Most of Dubai's leading hotels receive international news and entertainment via satellite. Star TV, Orbit, Showtime and FirstNet are among the satellite networks, which transmit a wide variety of programmes, including BBC World, CNN and Sky News. Locally, there are three channels: Dubai TV and Dubai Sports Channel, which show Arabic programmes, and Channel One TV, a family entertainment channel broadcasting terrestrially in English. A cable TV service entitled E-Vision is available in a number of areas in Dubai and combines a wide variety of Western and Eastern satellite channels. Programme details are published in the local press.

Transport

Currently taxis, municipal buses and *abras* (traditional water ferries) are the only forms of public transport, though most hotels have their own buses. Visitors and residents alike will find a variety of metered taxis that are clean and inexpensive.

With a view to improving the transportation system, the Dubai Metro project is well under way. The Dubai Metro will have three lines: the Red Line will run from the city to Jebel Ali via Dubai Marina, with its first phase scheduled to open in 2009; the Green Line will link strategic locations in the city, with its first phase scheduled to open in 2010; and the Blue Line will run from Dubai International Airport to Jebel Ali along Emirates Road, with its first phase scheduled to open in 2011. The Red and Green lines will have two interchange stations at Union Square and BurJuman. Ultimately the network could extend for 318 kilometres and will run underground in the city and on elevated viaducts elsewhere. In full operation, Dubai Metro is projected to carry 1.2 million passengers on an average day and the Red Line could eventually extend as far south as Abu Dhabi.

Videos and cinemas

Hotels have in-house movies and you'll find luxurious cinema complexes that screen English, Arabic and Hindi movies in abundance around the city.

Water

Tap water is desalinated and quite safe to drink, but many people prefer the inexpensive local mineral water that can be bought everywhere or delivered directly to your home. Locally bottled and international mineral waters are served in hotels.

Consulates and embassies

Most of the embassies are based in Abu Dhabi. The contact details of some Dubai-based consulates are as follows:

Angola, Consulate General of the Republic of: Tel 355 9041; e-mail
   angdubai@emirates.net.ae
Australian Consulate General: Tel 321 2444; e-mail info@austrade.gov.au
Bangladesh, Consulate General of: Tel 272 6966; e-mail bdoot@emirates.net.ae
British Embassy: Tel 309 4444; website www.britain-uae.org

Ski Dubai is the Middle East's first indoor ski slope and incorporates toboggan runs and attractions for children. A second ski slope is planned for Dubailand.

Canadian Consulate: Tel 314 5555; e-mail dubai@international.gc.ca

China, Consulate General of the People's Republic of: Tel 394 4733; e-mail chinaconsul_db_ae@mfa.gov.cn

Egypt, Consulate General of: Tel 397 1122; e-mail angdubai@emirates.net.ae

Ethiopia, Consulate General of: Tel 351 6868; e-mail ethcodu@ethcongen.ae

France, Consulate General of: Tel 332 9040; e-mail fransula@emirates.net.ae

Germany, Consulate General of the Federal Republic of: Tel 397 2333; e-mail info@dubai.diplo.de

India, Consulate General of: Tel 397 1333; e-mail cgidubai@emirates.net.ae

Iran, Consulate General of the Islamic Republic of: Tel 344 4717; e-mail iranconc@emirates.net.ae

Italy, Consulate General of: Tel 331 4167; e-mail secretariadubai@italsonsul.ae

Japan, Consulate General of: Tel: 331 9191; e-mail cgjapan@emirates.net.ae

Jordan, Consulate General of the Hashemite Kingdom of: Tel 397 0500; e-mail jorcnslt@emirates.net.ae

Kazakhstan, Consulate General of: Tel 224 2462; e-mail kzconuae@emirates.net.ae

Kuwait, Consulate General of the State of: Tel 397 8000; e-mail kuwaity@emirates.net.ae

Lebanon, Consulate General of: Tel 397 7450; e-mail lebconsd@emirates.net.ae

Libyan Consulate: Tel 397 3972; e-mail libyacon@hotmail.com

Malaysia, Consulate General of: Tel 335 5528/38; e-mail dubai@matrade.gov.my

New Zealand Consulate: Tel 331 7500; e-mail evelyn.mcnally@nzte.govt.nz

Pakistan, Consulate General of the Islamic Republic of: Tel 397 3600; e-mail parepdub@emirates.net.ae

Palestine, Consulate General of the State of: Tel 397 2020; e-mail falasteencons@hotmail.com

Panama, Consulate General of: Tel 337 2538; e-mail pancondb@emirates.net.ae

Qatar, Consulate General of: Tel 398 2888; e-mail qatar98@emirates.net.ae

Romania, Consulate General of: Tel 394 0580; e-mail romcons@emirates.net.ae

Royal Danish Consulate: Tel 348 0877; e-mail dtcdubai@emirates.net.ae

Royal Netherlands Consulate: Tel 352 8700; e-mail nlgovdba@emirates.net.ae

Royal Norwegian Consulate: Tel 353 3633; website www.norway.ae

Royal Thai Consulate General: Tel 349 2863; e-mail thaidub@emirates.net.ae

Russian Consulate: Tel 223 1272; e-mail conspred@emirates.net.ae

Saudi Arabia, Royal Consulate General of the Kingdom of: Tel 397 9188

Singapore, Consulate General of the Republic of: Tel 335 3770; e-mail sgconsdb@emirates.net.ae

Somalia, Consulate General of: Tel 295 8282

South Africa, Consulate of: Tel 397 5222; e-mail sacons@emirates.net.ae

Sri Lanka, Consulate General of: Tel 3986279; e-mail slcondxb@emirates.net.ae

Sudan, Consulate of: Tel 263 7555; e-mail sudancon@emirates.net.ae

Sultanate of Oman Office: Tel 397 1000; e-mail general@ocodubai.com

Switzerland, Consulate of: Tel 329 0999; e-mail vertretung@dai.rep.admin.ch

Syria, Consulate General of: Tel 266 3354; e-mail syrian-con-dubai@hotmail.com

Taiwan, Commercial Office of Republic of China: Tel 397 7888; e-mail corocdxb@emirates.net.ae

Turkish Consulate General: Tel 331 4788; e-mail tcdubkon@emirates.net.ae

United States of America, Consulate General of: Tel 311 6000; website http://dubai.usconsulate.gov

Uzbekistan, Consulate General of the Republic of: Tel 394 7400

Vietnam, Consulate General of: Tel 398 8924; e-mail vnconsul@emirates.net.ae

Yemen, Consulate of the Republic of: Tel 397 0131; e-mail gandan@emirates.net.ae

Burj Al Arab

PO Box 74147, Dubai, UAE
Tel: (+971 4) 301 7777   Fax: (+971 4) 301 7000
Email: BAAinfo@jumeirah.com   www.jumeirah.com

Rising from the Arabian Gulf on an island 280 metres from the shores of Jumeirah beach, stands the iconic Burj Al Arab, a masterpiece of contemporary architecture and the world's most luxurious hotel. Designed to resemble the graceful sails of an Arabian dhow, it soars to a height of 321 metres making it the tallest dedicated all-suite hotel in the world. Discreet in-suite check in, a private reception desk on every floor and a brigade of highly trained butlers providing round-the-clock attention, assure an unsurpassed personalised service to guests of the hotel. Adjacent to Madinat Jumeirah, Jumeirah Beach Hotel and Wild Wadi Waterpark, and in close proximity to Mall of the Emirates, Ski Dubai and an array of world-class golf courses, it is a perfectly situated landmark in the very heart of Dubai.

Emirates Al Maha Desert Resort & Spa

PO Box 7631, Dubai, UAE
Tel: (+971 4) 303 4222/4223   Fax: (+971 4) 343 9696
email: almaha@emirates.com   www.al-maha.com

Set in a 27-square-kilometre private reserve, just 45 minutes from cosmopolitan Dubai, Emirates Al Maha Desert Resort & Spa is an oasis of respite and natural beauty, a sanctuary for both man and beast, where the wonder of the desert combines with unsurpassed luxury. This exclusive suite-only resort accommodates a maximum of 74 guests and offers a unique Arabian heritage experience. A member of The Leading Small Hotels of the World, Emirates Al Maha provides unrivalled standards of service with a staff-to-guest ratio of 3:1. Each spacious, luxuriously appointed suite has its own deck and temperature-controlled pool offering uninterrupted views of the Hajar Mountains.

Emirates Marina Hotel & Residence

PO Box 7631, Dubai, UAE
Tel: (+971 4) 319 4000   Fax: (+971 4) 319 4006
Email: emiratesmarina@emirates.com   www.emirateshotelsresorts.com

Emirates Marina Hotel & Residence is part of the growing portfolio of Emirates Hotels & Resorts. Located in the prestigious Dubai Marina development, this 261 suite hotel offers staggering views of Palm Jumeirah Island and The Gulf. The luxurious studio, one-, two-, and three-bedroom suites and penthouses are ideal for short and long-term stays, whether for business or leisure. The hotel features three distinctive restaurants – Counter Culture, Azur and The Observatory. Emirates' own trademark Timeless Spa combines beauty and relaxation practices drawn from different cultures and healing disciplines. This is complemented by the exclusive range of Timeless products made from dates and frankincense.

The Fairmont Dubai

PO Box 97555, Dubai, UAE
Tel: (+971 4) 332 5555   Fax: (+971 4) 332 4555
Email: dubai.reservations@fairmont.com   www.fairmont.com

A distinctive landmark on the ever-evolving city skyline, The Fairmont Dubai is located in the business heart of the metropolis. The 34-storey property has extensive business and leisure facilities, with 394 rooms (including 128 suites), as well as its premium Fairmont Gold 'hotel within a hotel', 10 dining and entertainment venues, the Willow Stream Spa and two sundecks each with a mosaic-lined pool. State-of-the-art business technology is displayed throughout the hotel from the guest rooms to the 33rd-floor Executive Conference Centre, home to a 170-seat auditorium, and18 meeting rooms.

Grand Hyatt Dubai

PO Box 7978, Dubai, UAE
Tel: (+971 4) 317 1234   Fax: (+971 4) 317 1235
Email: reservations.grandhyattdubai@hyattintl.com
www.dubai.grand.hyatt.com

Grand Hyatt Dubai, a City Conference Resort, is a magnificent 674-room property near the shores of Dubai's creek. Four modern undulating structures make up the hotel, set within 37 acres of lavish gardens.
   Guestrooms and suites are decorated with luxurious fabrics and unique Middle Eastern artworks. All rooms offer superb views, looking towards the historic creek or Dubai's stunning city skyline.
   Grand Hyatt Dubai hosts the largest hotel conferencing facility in the region, along with nine restaurants, two bars, a coffee shop and a nightclub. The Grand Spa has luxury fitness facilities including squash courts, three outdoor pools and a Kidz Club.

Habtoor Grand Resort & Spa

PO Box 24454, Dubai, UAE
Tel: (+971 4) 399 5000   Fax: (+971 4) 399 4547
Email: grandjumeirah@habtoorhotels.com
www.habtoorhotels.com

Situated on Dubai's world famous Jumeirah Beach and adjacent to the magnificent Dubai Marina, the Habtoor Grand Resort & Spa occupies Dubai's most enchanting beachside location. There's a choice of 446 exceptional rooms and suites and the resort also boasts state of the art conference facilities. Pools, restaurants and bars are set amidst tropical gardens, the resort is a paradise of perfect vistas, where lush landscapes meet the warm Arabian Gulf, fringed by an immaculate beach and embraced by clear blue skies.

Hatta Fort Hotel

PO Box 9277, Dubai, UAE
Tel: (+971 4) 852 3211   Fax: (+971 4) 852 3561
Email: hfh@jaihotels.com www.jebelali-international.com

Dubai's Exclusive Mountain Retreat, the Hatta Fort Hotel, is an 80-acre, 50-room oasis of relaxation, offering the perfect break from the hustle and bustle of city life since it's just an hour's drive from Dubai. The Hatta Fort Hotel offers spacious accommodation overlooking the Hajar Mountains in the form of Chalet-Style and Deluxe Chalet-Style Rooms and Suites. Leisure facilities at the Hatta Fort Hotel includes two beautifully landscaped, temperature-controlled swimming pools, Senses Beauty Salon, a golf driving range, practice green, two floodlit tennis courts, indoor table tennis, billiards and mini-golf. A number of additional adventures like clay pigeon shooting, field and target archery, mountain biking and guided four-wheel drive mountain, desert and wadi excursions are also available.

Jebel Ali Golf Resort & Spa

PO Box 9255, Dubai, UAE
Tel: (+971 4) 883 6000   Fax: (+971 4) 883 5543
Email: jagrs@jaihotels.com www.jebelali-international.com

Situated on the golden shores of the Arabian Gulf, the Jebel Ali Golf Resort & Spa continuously combine its exquisite beauty with ultimate luxury and warm Arabian hospitality. In addition to the palm-lined private beach and three temperature-controlled swimming pools, the Resort also features a 9-hole championship standard golf course with golf academy, 80-berth marina, riding stables, a variety of different restaurants and bars and The Spa, a purpose-built wellness facility overlooking the beach. With suites and junior suites offering stunning views from spacious balconies and terraces, the Jebel Ali Golf Resort & Spa is truly a paradise for the discerning luxury traveller who enjoys privacy, exceptional service and complete relaxation.

Jumeirah Beach Hotel
PO Box 11416, Dubai, UAE
Tel: (+971 4) 348 0000   Fax: (+971 4) 301 6800
Email: JBHinfo@jumeirah.com   www.jumeirah.com

Architecturally ground breaking, this magnificent 26-storey hotel is designed to represent a breaking wave, with an interior based on the four elements of nature – earth, air, fire and water – culminating in a spectacular atrium which features a 90 metre high wall sculpture. All 598 rooms and 19 villas are sea facing and there's an array of land and water leisure facilities for adults and children. The health club, including gym, tennis courts, squash courts and sauna is built in the design of a nautilus shell and the conference centre in the shape of a dhow. The hotel houses more than 20 restaurants, cafes and bars as well as exclusive shops and has its own marina.

Jumeirah Emirates Towers
PO Box 72127, Dubai, UAE
Tel: (+971 4) 330 0000   Fax: (+971 4) 330 3030
Email: JETinfo@jumeirah.com   www.jumeirahemiratestowers.com

Recognized as the world's leading business hotel, Jumeirah Emirates Towers occupies a prime location in Dubai's most exciting commercial district and offers an ideal environment for the discerning corporate traveller. Yet with its stunning architecture, stylish 400 rooms and suites, an exclusive shopping boulevard and unique conference and meeting facilities, the hotel's appeal reaches far beyond the business world.

Guests may unwind at any of the two health clubs or outdoor swimming pool. Ladies staying on the Chopard Ladies Floor will enjoy complete privacy and exclusive amenities, whereas H_2O The Male Spa is a unique place for men seeking to de-stress and restore energy levels. The finest culinary standards await you at the 15 superb restaurants, lounges and bars.

JW Marriott Dubai
PO Box 16590, Dubai, UAE
Tel: (+971 4) 262 4444   Fax: (+971 4) 262 6264
Email: marriott@emirates.net.ae   www.jwmarriottdubai.com

The 351 spacious guest rooms including 52 suites of the JW Marriott Dubai are a haven of luxury and tranquillity in Dubai. The hotel has the largest skylight in the Middle East, below which nestles a magnificent town square surrounded by a variety of restaurants and bars. Visit the Asian-style Bamboo Lagoon, the international Market Place, the German Hofbräuhaus or the relaxing Piano Lounge. In the atrium lobby is the Italian Cucina restaurant, the JW's Steakhouse at the lower lobby and Champions Sports Bar adjacent to the Deira Ballroom. Griffins Health Club, with its squash courts and spa pool, and the terrace at the roof-top swimming pool, are other leisure options.

Kempinski Hotel Mall of the Emirates
PO Box 120679, Dubai, UAE
Tel: (+971 4) 341 0000   Fax: (+971 4) 341 4500
Email: reservations.malloftheemirates@kempinski.com
      www.kempinski-dubai.com

Located on Sheikh Zayed Road, the award winning hotel boasts Dubai's most spacious rooms and suites including 15 breathtaking ski chalets overlooking the ski slopes.

Hotel facilities include 24Seven restaurant, Aspen Café, 1897 Bar, Sezzam restaurant by the ski slopes, Spa, hairdresser, gym, swimming pool, tennis court, state of the art conference facilities, business centre and wireless hi speed internet connection. Personalized services such as shopping & pool butlers, baby sitting, in room spa treatments and video conferencing are on offer.

Le Meridien Mina Seyahi Beach Resort & Marina
PO Box 24883, Dubai, UAE
Tel: (+971 4) 399 3333   Fax: (+971 4) 399 3111
Email: reservations@lemeridien-minaseyahi.com
        www.lemeridien.com/minaseyahi

Whether for business or pleasure, Le Meridien Mina Seyahi offers superb facilities for all. Set in an idyllic landscape, on the shores of the Arabian Gulf, guests will find this modern, stylish five-star 211-room hotel exceeds all expectations. Water sports include deep-sea fishing, water skiing, windsurfing and sailing. For land-lovers, there is beach volleyball, beach football, tennis and a fully-equipped gymnasium with sauna. Relax and enjoy 500 metres of private beach, or simply laze around the sun-drenched pools. Le Meridien Mina Seyahi Beach Resort and Marina is all about lifestyle – action-packed, leisure-filled days and fun-filled nights of stylish chic at the seven restaurants and three popular bars.

The Metropolitan Palace Hotel
PO Box 56262, Dubai, UAE
Tel: (+971 4) 227 0000   Fax: (+971 4) 227 9993
Email: palacedubai@habtoorhotels.com

The hotel has 212 stylishly appointed rooms and suites and offers guests a vision of luxury, elegance & comfort. Perfect for both business and leisure, this 5-star boutique hotel is centrally located in Al Maktoum Street, the heart of Dubai's business district. Walking distance to the shopping malls, Dubai Creek, gold & spice souks, and minutes away from Dubai International Airport.

The Metropolitan Hotel
PO Box 26666, Dubai, UAE
Tel: (+971 4) 343 0000   Fax: (+971 4) 343 1146
Email: metdubai@habtoorhotels.com

Provides a wide array of facilities for guests with 192 tastefully decorated rooms and 63 deluxe fully furnished suites. The hotel also has 11 international bars and restaurants on site, and is superbly located in the heart of the rapidly growing business and commercial district of Sheikh Zayed Road. Just minutes away from Dubai International World Trade Centre and Exhibition Halls, with easy access to the Jebel Ali Free Zone, Media & Internet Cities and a short drive from Safa Park and the golden beaches of the Arabian Gulf.

Millennium Airport Hotel
PO Box 13018, Dubai, UAE
Tel: (+971 4) 282 3464   Fax: (+971 4) 282 0627
Email: sales.airdxb@mill-cop.com   www.millenniumhotels.com

Just two minutes from Dubai International Airport and at the crossroads of key routes to the city centre, Festival City, numerous parks, beaches and leisure districts. With 115 spacious deluxe and superior rooms, each equipped with satellite TV, electronic safe, IDD telephone and voicemail, and mini bar. The hotel also provides a range of facilities including baby sitting service on request, limousine service, complimentary underground car parking and tour reservations.

The Hotel's numerous dining and entertainment options include the award-winning restaurant Da Vinci's, the legendary English pub Biggles, Cactus Jack's Tex Mex and Gozo Garden all day dining restaurant.

Oasis Beach Hotel

PO Box 26500, Dubai, UAE
Tel: (+971 4) 399 4444   Fax: (+971 4) 399 4200
Email: obh@jaihotels.com   www.jebelali-international.com

The Oasis Beach Hotel offers a comprehensive array of leisure and business facilities combined with excellent service in a casual, tropical environment. Located on the Jumeirah Beach strip, adjacent to Dubai Marina, the Oasis Beach Hotel features 252 spacious, well-appointed rooms, Club rooms and Executive Sea View rooms. The Hotel has a large temperature-controlled swimming pool with swim up bar and a children's shallow pool, where kids can safely splash around. The wide selection of leisure facilities include land and water sports, a floodlit tennis court, state-of-the-art gym, sauna, Oasis Beach Beauty Salon and the Oasis Retreat, the Hotel's wellness centre. Two executive meeting rooms as well as a variety of excellent restaurants and bars are available.

Oasis Beach Tower

PO Box 26500, Dubai, UAE
Tel: (+971 4) 399 4444   Fax: (+971 4) 399 4200
Email: obt@jaihotels.com   www.jebelali-international.com

With its stately exuberance, the Oasis Beach Tower provides its residents with an unrivalled quality of life, no matter how long their stay. With direct access to the beach, incredible views over the Arabian Gulf and connection to full hotel services, this is a unique product that cannot be benchmarked against any other product in the region. In addition to spacious living areas, fully equipped kitchens and incredible views, all guests have access to full housekeeping services. With a glorious pool deck at the Oasis Beach Tower and private beach at the Oasis Beach Hotel to take advantage of, guests are spoilt for choice when it comes to leisure and recreation. Access to fitness and wellness facilities and an exceptional selection of dining options are also among the many benefits for guests.

Radisson SAS Hotel

PO Box 476, Dubai, UAE
Tel: (+971 4) 222 7171   Fax: (+971 4) 228 4777
Email: info.deiracreek.dubai@radissonsas.com
www.deiracreek.dubai.radissonsas.com

A five star luxury hotel in the heart of Dubai's bustling business district, The Radisson SAS Hotel, Dubai Deira Creek offers 287 rooms, all with balconies and fabulous views of the legendary Creek with a choice of 11 restaurants, 3 bars and Dhow and a Cake Shop.

With 13 different meeting rooms the hotel is ideal for small meetings and large conferences and weddings.

The hotel also includes a 24-hour Fitness Centre that features an outdoor swimming pool, tennis court, two squash courts, a fully-equipped gym with sauna and plunge pool, and massage rooms.

The Ritz-Carlton

PO Box 26525, Dubai, UAE
Tel: (+971 4) 399 4000   Fax: (+971 4) 399 4001
www.ritzcarlton.com

Built on the shores of the Arabian Gulf, The Ritz-Carlton, Dubai is an intimate retreat in the heart of Dubai Marina, overlooking 350 metres of white sandy beach and beautifully landscaped gardens. Architecture is a combination of Moorish and Islamic design; terra-cotta roof tiles with salmon hued exterior walls lend this resort an eclectic Mediterranean feeling. All 138 rooms and suites offer breathtaking views of the sea, and with 350 multi-cultural and multi-lingual employees, the hotel offers unparalleled levels of personalized service. Offering an array of fine dining options from formal to casual, with a choice of international and local cuisine. An authentic Balinese Spa offers a range of treatments. Additional facilities include a fitness centre, three pools, tennis, squash and nearby golf.

Rydges Plaza Hotel
PO Box 24621, Dubai, UAE
Tel: (+971 4) 398 2222   Fax: (+971 4) 398 3700
Email: info_dubai@rydges.ae   www.rydges.com/dubai

The Rydges Plaza is Dubai's premiere boutique hotel with 98 well-appointed rooms, offering personalized service and attention to detail that larger hotels are unable to provide. Extensive in room facilities; seven themed restaurants and two bars, function rooms capable of accommodating up to 200 guests, a state-of-the-art health club and swimming pool.

Coupled with our central location near Dubai World Trade Centre, the Jumeirah beachfront and just 15 minutes from the airport, we are able to offer a complete hospitality package to any Dubai visitor.

Shangri-La Hotel, Dubai
PO Box 75880, Dubai, UAE
Tel: (+971 4) 343 8888   Fax: (+971 4) 343 8886
Email: sldb@shangri-la.com   www.shangri-la.com

Set amongst the skyscrapers on Sheikh Zayed Road, Shangri-La Hotel, Dubai is an impressive 43-storey tower which has become one of the most prestigious addresses in Dubai with its 302 luxuriously appointed rooms and suites including 70 Horizon Club rooms and suites with a host of exclusive privileges and facilities including a private health club and an indoor infinity pool; 126 serviced furnished apartments in various options offering stunning city and ocean views; 9 food and beverage outlets offering international, seafood, French-Vietnamese, Cantonese and Moroccan cuisines; extensive recreation facilities including a health club and spa, outdoor swimming pool and tennis court; a 24-hour Business Centre and a choice of banquet venues including two ballrooms and three meeting rooms.

Sheraton Dubai Creek Hotel & Towers
PO Box 4250, Dubai, UAE
Tel: (+971 4) 228 1111   Fax: (+971 4) 221 3468
Email: dubai.creek@sheraton.com   www.sheraton.com/dubai

Centrally located, the charismatic Sheraton Dubai Creek Hotel & Towers is situated directly on the famous Dubai Creek, with easy access to the city's main commercial, shopping and recreational districts and just 7 kms from the airport.

262 rooms offer stunning views, broadband connectivity, in-room safe and more. Towers Floor guests are provided with personalized butler service, exclusive usage of the Towers Lounge, evening cocktails and more.

Dining experiences include Japanese, Italian, Indian and an English pub. The 5-star hotel also features a wide range of conference facilities and leisure amenities like gym, sauna/steam rooms, massage treatments, swimming pool and tennis.

The Westin Dubai Mina Seyahi Beach Resort & Marina
PO Box 24883
Tel: (+971 4) 399 3333   Fax: (+971 4) 399 3000
www.westin.com/dubaiminaseyahi

The Westin Dubai Mina Seyahi Beach Resort & Marina is a luxurious 5 star resort opening winter 2007/8. Located on the pristine Jumeirah Beach, the hotel offers 294 spacious guest rooms and suites with Heavenly Beds, luxurious bath amenities, Westin Workout fitness centre, a selection of contemporary and regional cuisine including Italian, Eastern and Steakhouse. Other sporting facilities include a meandering pool and a lap pool, 4 floodlit tennis courts and a Watersports Centre. An Italian designed conference centre with 7 state of the art venues, with a capacity from 14 to 5,000 guests, outdoor beachside amphitheatre, lawns and barbecue areas, make it the complete resort property.